Where Faith Seeks Understanding

Where Faith Seeks Understanding

Planning for Adult Education in the Church

MELVIN G. WILLIAMS

A Griggs Educational Resource
Abingdon Press
Nashville

Where Faith Seeks Understanding:
Planning for Adult Education in the Church

Copyright © 1987 by Abingdon Press

This book is printed on acid-free paper.

Library of Congress Cataloging-in-Publication Data

WILLIAMS, MELVIN GILBERT, 1937–
  Where faith seeks understanding.
  (A Griggs educational resource)
  Bibliography: p. 87
  1. Christian education of adults. I. Title.
  BV1488.W55   1987   268'.434   86-17309

ISBN 0-687-45173-6 (soft: alk. paper)

Scripture quotations noted JB are from the Jerusalem Bible, copyright © 1966 by Darton, Longman & Todd, Ltd. and Doubleday & Company, Inc. Used by permission of the publisher.

Scripture quotations noted RSV are from the Revised Standard Version of the Bible, copyrighted 1946, 1952, © 1971, 1973 by the Division of Christian Education of the National Council of the Churches of Christ in the U.S.A., and are used by permission.

Chapter 1 adapted from Melvin G. Williams, "The Second Hour: Where Faith Seeks Understanding," *The Christian Ministry* (November 1984). Copyright 1984 The Christian Century Foundation.

Pages 54-56 adapted by permission from "A Cry from the Cross," Melvin G. Williams, *JED Share* (Spring 1985). Copyright © 1985 by United Church Press.

Pages 57-58 adapted from "Blessed Are You Who Listen," Melvin G. Williams, *A.D.* (February 1983). By permission of *A.D.*

Pages 72-74 adapted from "How to Tell the Children," Melvin G. Williams, *Catholic Digest* (April 1986). Copyright © 1986 by the College of St. Thomas, reprinted by permission of author.

MANUFACTURED BY THE PARTHENON PRESS AT
NASHVILLE, TENNESSEE, UNITED STATES OF AMERICA

TO MARCIE . . .

. . . *Who Knows Why*

Acknowledgments

My debts are many and it is a pleasure to acknowledge some of the most significant among them here:

- to the members and staff of the First Congregational Church in Bloomfield, Connecticut, for *stimulating* my thinking,
- to Jackson W. Carroll, David A. Roozen, and Audrey Miller for both *broadening* and *focusing* my thinking, and
- to Marcie Williams, for *encouraging* my thinking.

My thanks to all.

Ideas are clean. They soar in the serene supernal. I can take them out and look at them, they fit in books, they lead me down that narrow way. And in the morning they are there. Ideas are straight—

But the world is round, and a
messy mortal is my friend,

Come walk with me in the mud. . . .

—Hugh Prather

Contents

Preface

Adults have been receiving a Christian education for almost 250 years at the First Congregational Church in Bloomfield, Connecticut—ever since the church was founded in 1738. That would have been inevitable, of course, since some sort of learning—intended or not—would have resulted from each activity of the congregation, from participating in worship to planning the budget to preparing a chicken supper. In recent years, however, adult education has begun to receive a significantly greater degree of attention than it has been given historically—deliberate attention that has been reflected variously in the assignment of professional staff time, in the organization of the Christian Education Committee, and in the availability of courses for the congregation.

This congregation and this new sense of priority provided the context for a project which was designed to explore with adults how they can and do learn in the contemporary church, especially in the second hour on Sunday mornings, and to prepare them to take more responsibility for adult education in their congregation. All of the components of the project, from its planning to its evaluation, can be adapted to the needs and opportunities of other congregations as well.

Who will find it useful? Any who are committed to expanding adult education in the church, especially in a way that will place the Christian community squarely at the intersection of religious tradition and contemporary life, and to enlarging the role of laity both in and beyond the local congregation in a way that will make mutual ministry more an experience than a hope.

THE WIDER CONTEXT

Several assumptions lie behind this undertaking: (1) that all Christians are called to minister in the world, (2) that the local church is responsible for providing its adult members with learning experiences designed to meet both intellectual and emotional needs, and (3) that while learning can and does happen everywhere in the church, Christian education for adults should include elements that are intentional and structured.

Moreover, because education is a social as well as a personal experience, it is appropriate both that Christian education be offered in controlled social contexts and that it be lived out in the larger culture. The second hour study session, following the faith experience of worship, can be the ideal context in which faith can seek understanding. In addition, it can be an opportunity for lay men and women to be both informed and empowered for ministry.

The criteria for such an approach grow out of an understanding (following Anselm and others) that adult education in the church is primarily a response to faith rather than a cause of it. Also, I believe that adult education in the church can be both a place for reflection and a base for action.

A PERSONAL WORD

For more than twenty-five years I have been a teacher, a scholar, and a writer, devoting most of my professional career to the world of literature and the humanities. Since 1961 I have been a member of the English Department of American International College, Springfield, Massachusetts. For much of this time I have also been involved in Christian education at the local church level. This book draws upon my experience and skills in communication, in educational theory, and in the psychology of adult behavior. It also applies my study of contemporary theology, of leadership styles, of the church as a covenant community, and of the sociology of knowledge.

Published resources on which the book are built (see bibliography) include those which recognize creative opportunities for lay ministries and which offer insights into the behavior of adult learners. Personal and organizational resources include not only the ministerial staff at the Bloomfield Congregational Church but also its lay leadership who are deeply committed to an enlarged emphasis on adult education.

Since writing this book I have accepted a call to a new position as Minister of Education at the Federated Community Church in Hampden, Massachusetts.

Where
Faith Seeks
Understanding

CHAPTER ONE

Introduction

Imagine a two-track course of study:
one that starts with *now* and moves back to *then*,
the other that starts with *then* and
moves up to *now*.

Three red letters—KKK—dominated the top of the pad of newsprint as about three dozen persons, adults plus a few teenagers, gathered in the church's living room. It was 11:15 on a Sunday morning, following the worship service, and this was the second-hour class.

"I'd like to invite each of you to begin thinking about our issue for this month's series," the leader opened, "by playing a word game—a word association game. See those three red letters—KKK? What words do they bring to your mind? Call them out and we'll put them on the pad."

"Evil . . . Racist . . . Burning Crosses . . . Fear . . . Here." The list quickly grew to about twenty items as one person after another began to participate. The leader repeated each word as it was suggested, and he wrote it down. But he made no attempt to explain or to question or to comment.

"Good so far," he affirmed. "Now that's been a way to look at the Klan from the outside—from our side, the usual way we would expect to see such an organization. But let's look at our list of words again. Are there any, do you suppose, that Klan members might have come up with themselves? If you see any possibilities, we'll circle those in another color."

A kind of restless silence took hold for a moment, but then someone said "Racist" and another followed with "Here." "How about 'Crosses,' " a third queried. "Or do you suppose they'd say 'Christian' instead?"

By then—ten to fifteen minutes after the class had begun—more than half of the group had gotten actively involved. At first the lines of communication had gone back and forth from the leader to the individual participants, but the group soon created its own design: assent, affirmation, inquiry, disagreement, illustration. The leader's role was always important, but this morning he was not the primary source of information. He was there to help the group to learn from one another. He was an enabler.

It was 11:30 by then, a third of the way into the available time. The leader's role shifted a little as he wrote on the pad three brief questions about the Klan: *Why? Why here? Why now?*

The group was already working well together, so this time the responses flowed easily. The leader would sometimes comment, would often briefly summarize, and each time would write on the pad of newsprint.

What was going on? Adult education, in a form which offers the best opportunity for many

K K K

FEAR

CROSSES —

　　　　CHRISTIAN?

EVIL!

HERE!

congregations today. Men and women in all denominations are talking about empowering the laity, about mutual ministry, and about the need to provide continuing education for adults. Many want to combine all these in a way that will place the local Christian community at the intersection of tradition and contemporary life.

The second-hour study group can be a way to make these goals come alive.

Take a behind-the-scenes look at what was happening in this group by briefly exploring three areas: how adults learn, how they learn in the second-hour format, and what subjects can best be investigated there.

How do adults learn? We learn when we are solving problems that matter to us personally. Unlike school children, who may tolerate learning something simply because it is required of them and who may remember it only long enough to pass a test, most adults prefer to learn in more practical ways. Why learn to speak French? Because we plan to host an exchange student from Paris for a year and then spend the summer with her in Europe. That solves a personal problem. Why learn to operate the new word processor? Because we need to get reports and other mailings out more quickly. That solves a professional problem. Why learn what the opportunities are to provide better rental housing for low-income families in the community? Because we wish to act on their behalf, perhaps with an advocacy program or with lobbying efforts to change local building codes. That solves a social problem.

The principle is simple: education for adults, whether inside or outside the church, is most successful when it challenges the learners not simply to change what they *know* but to change what they *do*.

How does the second-hour session help? Educators have understood for a long while that, generally, learning is as much a social as a personal activity. That is, we learn as members of a family, a school, a community, a church. Though that is true at any time, it is especially significant when we come to a second-hour class. We are at the high point that follows a worship experience in which we have participated with one another as a community of faith and in which we have been challenged to live as sons and daughters of God. What better preparation could there be to grapple with problem-centered learning?

A flexible schedule should be provided, allowing either a one-time program or a series that runs for several weeks, and thus permitting an easy flow of participants in and out of the group. A few persons will stick with adult education as often as the classroom doors are open, especially since they are already in church anyway. But all will stay only when the focus of the course illuminates their own problems. At other times they may choose to go to the coffee hour instead, or to go home.

Finally, *what subjects can best be explored during second-hour classes?* Imagine a two-track course of study: one that starts with *now* and moves back to *then*, the other that starts with *then* and moves up to *now*. In a large church, both might operate at the same time with different groups. In a smaller church they might alternate. Either way, however, the focus is on the sort of Christian education that comes alive at the intersection of the traditions of faith with the experiences of the world around us.

Study church creeds?—yes. But journey toward the goal of developing a working creed for each learner individually as well as for the group or for the larger congregation. Address the pressing social issues of the community?—of course. But act on housing for the poor, or justice for minorities, or peace in the world, not in the same way that the housing commission or the peace coalition does. Act instead as the light of faith reflects on the road ahead.

The second-hour format (the time after worship on Sunday morning) will not be right for every congregation. Alternatives for these congregations could be weekend retreats or mid-week classes, though the dynamics of Christian education are different at these times. Also, the *second*-hour class cannot work in quite the same way when a church meets for worship at eleven o'clock. A "first hour" may then be a useful alternative, or a "middle hour" when there are two worship services. Still, the second-hour session remains one of the most attractive of all opportunities to fulfill Reinhold Niebuhr's dream for Christian education: that it be the place "where faith seeks understanding" (Niebuhr, p. 125).

Activities for Teachers and Learners

REFLECTION ON THE READING

The study guide which follows each chapter begins with a three-part comprehension check designed to guide readers toward a full understanding. (See the statement by Harold E. Herber at the end of the exercise.) One can respond to the questions individually, of course, but the activity will be more effective if several readers work together.

I. Directions: Listed below are three statements. Review the chapter you have just read to see if it contains the same information that you find here. It does not matter whether the words are identical or are paraphrased, but there must be evidence somewhere in the chapter to support your opinion. Respond to all three statements.

	Agree	Disagree
1. Adults learn best in order to pass tests.	——	——
2. Adults learn best in groups.	——	——
3. Adults learn best right after a worship service.	——	——

II. Directions: Read through the following statements and think about how they relate to the information in the preceding chapter. Check each statement which expresses an idea that can be reasonably supported with information from the reading. Be ready to discuss the supporting evidence with another reader.

—— 1. The Ku Klux Klan is a Christian organization because it uses the cross in its rituals.

—— 2. It's better for an adult teacher to ask for information than to provide it.

—— 3. Education in church is a problem.

III. Directions: Read through the following statements. Think about ideas and experiences you have had which are similar in principle to those you read about in the preceding chapter. Check each statement which you think is reasonable and which you can support by combining ideas in the reading selection with your own related ideas and experiences. Be ready to present evidence from both sources to support your decisions.

—— 1. Adult education in the church should always be Bible-centered.

—— 2. "Christian education" is "education for Christians."

—— 3. "Train up a child in the way he should go and when he is old he will not depart from it."

ACTION ON THE READING

Check Out Your Own Adult Education Program

1. Who makes the decisions about adult education in your church? List five persons, in order of importance:

   a. _____
   b. _____
   c. _____
   d. _____
   e. _____

2. How are adult education programs publicized? _____
   _____
   _____

3. Who teaches adult education classes?

   a. Most often: _____
   b. Fairly often: _____
   c. Now and then: _____

4. What formats do you use?

   a. First hour (before worship on Sunday) _____
   b. Second hour (after worship on Sunday) _____
   c. Weekdays, during the day _____
   d. Weekdays, at night _____
   e. Retreats _____
   f. Special seasons: _____   Advent series _____   Lenten series _____
   g. Other _____

5. List four recent adult education activities, and beside each indicate the need(s) which it met for those who participated.

   Activity: Need:

   a. _____   _____
   b. _____   _____
   c. _____   _____
   d. _____   _____

6. What are your hopes and dreams for adult education in your church:

 a. For yourself: ————————————————————————————
 ——
 ——

 b. For one other person: ——————————————————————
 ——
 ——

 c. For the church as an institution: ——————————————
 ——
 ——

 d. For your community: ————————————————————————
 ——
 ——

Harold E. Herber on reading comprehension:

"Reading comprehension can be simplified by defining it as a three-level process. First, the reader examines the words of the author and determines what is being said, what information is being presented.

"Second, the reader looks for relationships among statements within the materials, and from these intrinsic relationships derives various meanings. . . .

"Third, the reader takes the product of the literal—what the author has said—and the interpretive—what the author meant by what he said—and applies it to the knowledge she already possesses, thereby deepening the understanding" (Herber, pp. 39-40).

CHAPTER TWO

Adults Ought to Know Better

The church needs to educate its laity; that is clear. Now
more than ever before, the climate is right.

FAITH SEEKS UNDERSTANDING

The experience of faith precedes the awareness of faith. That is both the declaration of
Scripture and the witness of God's people everywhere.

In the book of Jeremiah, Yahweh promises that with the coming of the new covenant a law
will be set within his people, written on their hearts. Specifically, the text declares, "No
longer shall each man teach his brother, saying, 'Know the Lord,' for they shall all know me,
from the least of them to the greatest" (Jeremiah 31:34 RSV). Later the New Testament
writers portray such a relationship as existing within a specifically Christian context,
describing faith as "not your own doing" but as "the gift of God" (Ephesians 2:8 RSV).

Yet only with maturity have men and women, from biblical times to our own, also become
aware of their faith—that set of glasses through which they view themselves and the world
(Lewis, p. 7). Only then have they become able to assert it, to examine it, and to understand it.

A familiar example from the Old Testament text is the experience of the anonymous writer
of the Twenty-second Psalm, in whose expression of both faith and anguish we find a truth
that endures. When the poet cries out, "My God, my God, why have you forsaken me?" his
faith experience of "My God" precedes his plea to understand why. This is more than a
literary device or an accident of syntax. For him as for us, faith comes before understanding.
More than that, faith seeks understanding.

This is evident in the life of the psalmist and for any of us who pray his prayer as our own, at
a personal level. But it can also be the corporate experience of an entire congregation for
whom the response of faith in worship is quite separate from, and prior to, their quest for
understanding. Worship is the central expression of the life of faith and thus it is the central
activity of Christian churches. But it is not the whole activity of any congregation, nor should
it be. As adults we wish—and need—to learn about both the roots of our faith and its
implications for our daily life.

The idea that *faith seeks understanding* lies at the foundation of this study in a particular
way, for it is in the activities of adult education, particularly when conducted during the
second-hour session on a Sunday morning, that the phrase achieves its richest meaning for
many Christians.

THE IMPORTANCE OF ADULTS IN THE CHURCH

Many persons speak of children as the future of the church and certainly they are, in some
obvious ways. It is even more true, though, that adults are the future of the church. We are its

leaders, we are the ones who serve on its boards and committees, and we are the most influential in the life of the community. What we adults learn and do in our faith journeys determines not only what the church is now but what it will be when our children are at an age to take responsibility for themselves. One writer summarizes, "A church is essentially . . . an adult institution" (Zuck, p. 9). And another adds, "the church's ministry to children is only as effective as its adult education" (Hainer, p. 1).

CURRENT INFLUENCES ON ADULT EDUCATION IN THE CHURCH

Currently, two trends are having a particularly strong influence on this quest for understanding in the life of faith: the continuing emphasis on lifelong learning, and the growing recognition that mutual ministry in the world is the proper role for the laity.

Lifelong Learning

No one would disagree that a dozen years of required schooling cannot begin to provide sufficient education for adults today. Even university and graduate studies are not enough. Useful as they are, these experiences cannot equip a person for a lifetime of opportunities and decisions, many of which could not have been foreseen even a few years ago. So by the thousands, men and women are continuing to learn, deliberately and effectively.

Many of them attend classes where they gain academic credit as well as useful skills. Ever-increasing requirements for credentials and continuing professional education make it necessary for some to go this route. Nurses and accountants, to cite only two examples, must complete not only extensive studies to enter their career fields but also dozens of hours of classroom study every year to remain in good standing among their colleagues.

But continuing education in this country also means something more than taking courses in formal academic settings. Many who have no interest whatsoever in college credits or upgraded credentials are "looking for new sources of satisfaction and meaning in their lives, especially as they grow older" (Peterson, p. 2). For some, to be sure, this quest may appear largely on the fringes of their lives: perhaps learning to tie flies or do counted cross-stitch. For others, though, it may be more central, perhaps in support groups for young parents or in hospice volunteering among the elderly.

Either way, however, one point is clear: that "the center of educational gravity in society is shifting away from educational institutions toward informal learning, continuing education outside of school in the community, and self-learning without formal structures or conventional teachers" (Hesburgh, p. xi).

The implications of this shift for the church are hopeful, even exciting. Not only does it create an atmosphere that recognizes and supports the need for adult education, it also challenges the church to explore alternative structures and strategies of education.

We have known for years that people like to learn in church. Recently that awareness has been supported by statistical surveys. One of them concludes: "The overwhelming fact remains: for hundreds of thousands of people . . . the church is the single most preferred, most comfortable setting outside the home for almost any organized activity" (Peterson, pp.

CONTEMPORARY
EDUCATION

INFORMAL
LEARNING

ACADEMIC
SETTINGS

45-49). Add to that the fact that churches "far outnumber all the other types of community organizations" (ibid.) and the scope of the opportunity grows large indeed.

Declining attendance by almost all but older women in mainline churches may seem to lessen the opportunities for Christian education; let us face that squarely. Yet at the same time the fact of those trends makes more intense the challenges of addressing the needs of those who do participate.

The church needs to educate its laity; that is clear. Now more than ever before, the climate is right.

Mutual Ministry: A Larger Role for the Laity

A second positive influence on adult education in the church is the growing understanding of what ministry means. Some persons speak of "mutual ministry" (Fenhagen), others of "shared ministry," still others of "Monday's ministries" (Vos). But whatever the language, ministry is perceived today as a partnership of all Christians, both lay and ordained, functioning in varied settings in the world.

Even so, it sometimes has seemed easier to define what the laity are not than what they are, easier to describe what they do not do than what they do.

Everyone knows, of course, what laypersons are not. They are not professionally trained clergy. And what don't they do? They do not preach on Sunday morning—at least not very often. They never pronounce any others in the congregation husband and wife. They don't wear black shirts with uncomfortable-looking backward collars. And they don't usually have their names listed as "minister" on the signboard in front of the church building (though I have seen more than one such sign proclaim: "Ministers—All the Members of This Church" (Williams, "On the Laity," pp. 7, 9).

Even the dictionary customarily defines a layperson in terms that are negative, as "one not belonging to some particular profession" or "one who does not have special or advanced training or skill." The best it can do is to speak of such a person as "a member of the congregation as distinguished from the clergy" (ibid.).

In the contemporary church, fortunately, such negative approaches are being replaced by others that describe both the mutuality of ministry and, at the same time, the unique roles of both clergy and laity. "Minister" is slowly coming to be understood as a verb describing actions that all Christians are engaged in, as well as a noun that identifies the professional leader of a congregation.

Perhaps the most widely reported illustration of this emphasis is the Laity Project, which began at Andover Newton Theological School in 1977 and continues there as the Center for the Ministry of the Laity. But seminaries and lay academies and study groups in many places are exploring the calling of the laity under course titles as varied as "Mutual Ministry," "Sharing the Pastoral Office," "Ministry in the Marketplace," and "Ministry Support Groups."

Wherever they are held, the function of such courses is essential, not only to *explain* such

ideas but in the process to *equip* the laity for their dual roles in the world and in the workplace (see chapter 4).

The theology is clear: that servanthood is to be not only the style of leadership in the entire Christian community but also its mark of ministry. One layman goes so far as to insist, "The biblical and theological principle of all Christians being called into ministry is so clear that it is not even debated in the church" (Diehl, p. 14).

Still, the struggle continues as Christians try to define appropriate forms of partnership between clergy and laity. "There is good reason to celebrate the growing willingness of the institutional church to affirm the full ministry of all people," Richard R. Broholm maintains. But he continues, "Nevertheless, the task of actually claiming and identifying our ministry in the workplace is, for most of us, exceedingly difficult" (Broholm, p. 1).

Some persons, meanwhile, feel that it is still necessary to affirm a strong theology of the laity. A resolution passed in 1985 by the Connecticut Conference of the United Church of Christ, for instance, was intended to clarify the use of the word "minister" itself.

"Common usage," the resolution asserts, "has led to confusion of the term 'minister' so that it now connotes [only] ordained Protestant clergy." Yet, it continues, "all Christians need to be aware that we are ministers, called to continue Christ's ministry in the countless, concrete acts of making God present in our world as we are given the gift, wherever we are, of living in relationship with others." It declares, finally, "that the word 'minister' shall refer to baptized Christians in all publications of the Connecticut Conference; and that this practice be commended to our Connecticut Churches and to the United Church of Christ" (United Church of Christ, *Resolutions*).

This proposal appeared, it needs to be pointed out, a full quarter of a century after the founding in 1957 of the United Church of Christ, whose constitution proclaims that "the privilege and responsibility of witnessing to the gospel belongs to every member of the church" (United Church of Christ, *Constitution and Bylaws*). The denomination's General Synod, in 1973, created the Office for Church Life and Leadership, a structure designed specifically to enable and support the ministries of all of its members. But it was in the same year that both the United Church of Christ and the World Council of Churches devoted considerable time to similar questions in their delegate assemblies.

So the debate continues. And it should.

Among other indications that such a discussion still needs to be carried out is the inclusion of an unfortunate analogy—the image of the priest as wagon master on the frontier—in a recent book by the late Urban T. Holmes. Writing about "spirituality for ministry," Holmes portrays the ordained clergy as having not only a different kind of leadership role from the laity but—and this is the problem—a superior role. In fact, he portrays the laity as not being leaders at all, but only courageous adventurers at best.

In the following description, read "priest" as well as "wagon master" for "he":

> His qualification was that he had been over the trail before, he knew where the water holes were and where the Indians might attack. The wagon master did not drive the wagons and all the

travelers had to shoot for themselves. Each person's motives for being on that quest were their own and not his business. He had courage and commitment, but there were no guarantees of getting to California (Holmes, p. 186).

The analogy is clever and, no doubt offers an accurate portrayal of some of the role differences that do exist between priest and people. In fairness, too, it ought to be pointed out that this description comes out of an episcopal rather than a free church perspective. But even so, its publication by a respected writer, educator, and priest makes all too fuzzy the implications of the Reformation belief in the priesthood of all believers—that is, of all those who are "on the trail." Thus it obscures rather than clarifies the dimensions of shared ministry to which so many Christians are committed.

More Than Doorkeepers

To be a Christian is to minister; that sounds simple enough. To "increase the love of God and neighbor"—that is H. Richard Niebuhr's well-known description of what it means to minister (Niebuhr, p. 27). Yet in practice, as we have seen already, it is not so simple to know just what the relationships ought to be between lay and ordained ministers, or to know how all Christians can do Christ's ministry in their lives. And even then, there is a large gap between knowing and doing.

Some things we have learned, however.

We have come a long way, for instance, since it was supposed that laypersons should serve primarily in traditional areas within the church itself: collecting the offering or seating the latecomers, chaperoning the youth fellowship retreat or teaching in the primary department, scrambling the eggs for Lenten breakfasts or reshelving books in the church library, serving on committees or taking communion to shut-ins.

Few persons would wish to rule out such participation in the life of the church; many continue to find it meaningful and fulfilling. But if service within, not beyond, the institution is all that any Christians offer, then their horizons are certainly too narrow. Described in negative terms by one layman, "It is nothing short of a scandal when we in the church so limit our vision of ministry that we cannot see it extending beyond the walls of our own congregations" (Diehl, p. 14). Or expressed more positively (to return to the language of the resolution cited above), "The whole people of God, the Laos, are called to make incarnate our faith, to be the presence, the Body, of Christ in the world every day of the week, wherever we are, and to share fully in Christ's ministry" (United Church of Christ).

Ministry in the Workplace

"Wherever we are"—that is the key to the contemporary emphasis. What we are seeing is a growing understanding that laity, while they are every bit as much "ministers" as the ordained clergy, have a unique role as Christians which goes well beyond serving the institutional needs of the church and, in particular, beyond helping the pastor. It also goes beyond the social action roles that marked the sixties and seventies.

One recent statement expresses well the scope of this sort of ministry: "We are being encouraged to discover that ministry is also related to our workday roles as tool and die makers, nurses, public school teachers, accountants, bank managers, and homemakers. We are being asked to think of our faith not simply as a part-time affair focused largely on what we do within the gathered Christian community, but fundamentally as the way we experience and incarnate what we believe about God and God's world in the whole round of daily activities, incuding what we commonly refer to as our workplace" (Broholm, p. 1).

Is it true, meanwhile, that most laity still continue to think of themselves as the recipients rather than the agents of ministry? Do many still associate the life of the church more closely "with their place of residence rather than their place of work, with residential and family life rather than with work life[?] . . . Symbolically, as well as physically, [is] the church bell . . . seldom heard where a man earns his daily bread"? (Ernsberger, p. 55) Some of the evidence, at least, suggests that it still is. Although the destination is becoming more clear, the journey toward mutual ministry has barely begun.

FOUR P's OF ADULT EDUCATION IN THE CHURCH

The empowering of the laity is changing many things in the contemporary church, but probably none of them more than adult education. Its goals are changing, its strategies are changing, and its participants are changing.

We are fortunate to have put considerable distance between ouselves and "the formal educational experience of the great majority of adults in the church" almost two decades ago, which conveyed to them the general impression "that Christian education for adults principally amounts to training in how to perform various church jobs" (Ernsberger, p. 19). Yet how are we to translate the principles of mutual ministry into practice in our local churches and communities, and beyond? That is still a pressing issue.

Four simple assertions can be made, meanwhile, as a foundation upon which to erect a structure of lay education in the local church. Adult education is *possible,* first of all. Then, to be effective it ought to be both *personal* and *problem-centered.* And finally, its impact can be *powerful* indeed.

Possible

Most adults not only want to learn and can learn but also *enjoy* learning. And they find the church to be a supportive and value-laden place in which to do it. It is true that they are probably learning most of the time they are in church anyway, if they are at all alert, but they can also be drawn into the fellowship of those who "seek understanding" in a regular, structured way. The denominational staffer who confessed to me not long ago that "our churches aren't doing very much with adult education, not on Sundays anyway" was describing honestly his frustration with the life of his own fellowship. But he was not lifting his eyes to the peaks of possibility being reached in hundreds of other churches across the land.

Adult education is more than possible; it's happening.

Personal

How to make that process of adult education work successfully is neither easy nor automatic, of course. No formula is available; no bit of software will run itself with a simple keystroke. But an essential first step is to believe that the learners themselves are the reason for the programs, that adult education in the church is self-discovery before it is the mastery of facts or skills.

Personal—that is the focus.

In this regard, David Ernsberger's words are just as appropriate now as they were when he wrote them almost twenty years ago. "The church is of immense value as servant to the world," he asserts, "in simply providing opportunities for reflective thinking and the exchange of significant ideas and feelings, inasmuch as this kind of vital conversation is so often crowded out both at work and at home by daily crises and deadlines, and by escapist small talk that skirts encounters with life's deeper issues" (Ernsberger, p. 105).

Problem-centered

Possible first, then personal. What else?

Ask almost any group of adults what they have most enjoyed learning, or what educational experiences they have found most valuable, and expect to hear them describe something that solved a problem. It could have been a major problem: how to cope with the infirmities of aging parents. Or a smaller one: how to make this summer's vacation more interesting than last year's. For the first, establishing a support group with other "sandwich generation" couples might have been the start of a valuable experience. For the second, it might have been learning to hang-glide or do watercolors. The point here is not to identify a host of possible problems but to recognize that adult education which starts with personal problems in need of solving rather than with impersonal ideas in need of studying is more likely to bear fruit.

Unfortunately, the church has not often enough approached adult education this way. Hear the complaint of a layperson who recalls, "Our adult studies programs usually started with Bible study or teachings of the church. We were then expected to find 'practical applications' for these teachings." And then hear his suggestion: "It would have been much more helpful if the study programs would have started with the real-life situations facing the people at that time and then brought in the appropriate Bible studies or theology which related to them. What does our faith have to say about competition, for example? We can point to the evils of an excessively competitive society but when do we deal with a theology of competition, per se? Yet all of us are daily involved in competition—in school, jobs, sports, life styles, performing arts—you name it" (Diehl, p. 14).

If competition is not the pressing issue, there are other areas of modern life for adult study groups to consider, ranging from sexuality to stress to stewardship. Other approaches address the heritage and traditions of the church from a problem-solving perspective: trying

33

to decide, for instance, why the heroic stories of Esther and Judith both appear in early Christian literature even though only the story of Esther is found in the canon of Hebrew Scriptures. But be forewarned that this more academic and historic kind of study is likely to be more successful when it reflects somone's actual question and is not just a clever title for a traditional class.

To make adult education in the church so directive, one must concede, may not only risk an unfortunate narrowing of the entire learning process but may also seem to abandon the experience of learning for its own sake. Certainly anyone who recalls Aristotle's classic distinction between liberal and illiberal education knows that not all education needs to be either functional or predictable. Morris Keeton, for instance, cautions that "the very heart of learning is . . . a process in which unexpected things emerge" (Keeton, p. 147). John Dewey, too, has insisted that our "ends-in-view" be tentative, to allow for "the possibility that what we learn may itself change our purposes as learners" (Smythe, p. 5).

But Christian education that is problem-centered need be neither illiberal nor constrained, for what is controlled are the learners' points of origin rather than their destinations. Genuine problem-solving, after all, seeks answers that are unknown.

The local church is neither a college nor a seminary, and its educational mission is neither broad cultural awareness nor vocational specialization. Rather, it exists to equip Christians for ministry in the world. Using a problem-search model is not the only way to achieve this readiness, but it is certainly among the most fruitful.

Powerful

And what will be the result of this kind of adult education? At its best, in my experience, it will be change. There will be more than just changed knowledge, there can be changed relationships and changed actions. There can even be transformation. To be sure, not all changes are very dramatic, but even at the most pedestrian levels, change can be both lasting and powerful.

THE FIFTH 'P'—PRIORITY

Having said this much, one must nonetheless concede that continuing education for adults does not yet have a sufficiently high priority in the church. A 1972 study reported only 29 percent of all churches having any program to educate adults (Peterson, p. 14). In that same year Jerold Apps wrote, "The church touches more adults in a week than any other institution, yet it does little with them" (Apps, p. 13).

Ten years later a survey of "adult Christian learning" in the United Presbyterian Church in the U.S.A. continued to show disappointing statistics. While only 15 percent of members and pastors reported "nothing at all in this area," more "disheartening" was the report that a quarter of all members who responded to the survey were so unaware of possible adult learning opportunities in their churches that they were unable to report at all. Further, more than three out of five members in those churches that did offer adult education programs

34

reported either never attending them at all or, at best, going only "several times a year" ("Presbyterian Panel Findings").

It should come as no surprise then that Barbara Wheeler, president of Auburn Seminary, recently described "theological education for lay adults" as "the most profoundly neglected activity in most churches" (Wheeler, p. 5).

But it does not have to be that way.

My experience is that Christian education for adults can be attractive, even exciting. It can be that way on a weekend retreat at a ski lodge, of course, or on a windjammer cruise along the Maine coast. It can be that way at an executives' weekly luncheon called "Conversations Sandwiched In" or at an evening support group for singles called "Prime Time."

And it can be that way, too, during the second hour on Sunday morning.

Activities for Teachers and Learners

REFLECTION ON THE READING

I. Directions: Listed below are three statements. Review the chapter you have just read to see if it contains the same information that you find here. It does not matter whether the words are identical or are paraphrased, but there must be evidence somewhere in the chapter to support your opinion. Respond to all three statements.

	Agree	Disagree
1. The experience of faith precedes the awareness of faith.	——	——
2. A dozen years of required schooling provide sufficient education for adults today.	——	——
3. Most of the people who go to church these days are old women.	——	——

II. Directions: Read through the following statements and think about how they relate to the information in the preceding chapter. Check each statement which expresses an idea that can be reasonably supported with information from the reading. Be ready to discuss the supporting evidence with another reader.

—— 1. Learning *in churches* stands a greater chance of success for adults than learning almost anywhere else.

—— 2. Ministers are better described as "shepherds" than as "wagon masters."

—— 3. Lay Christians are discovering the need to be more than doormats in the church.

III. Directions: Read through the following statements. Think about ideas and experiences you have had which are similar in principle to those you read about in the preceding chapter. Check each statement which you think is reasonable and which you can support by combining ideas in the reading selection with your own related ideas and experiences. Be ready to present evidence from both sources to support your decisions.

—— 1. Analogies are never perfect, but they're often creative ways to try to understand something complex.

—— 2. No church is an island.

—— 3. It's time to get rid of the word "sanctuary" as a label for the main room where Christians gather on Sunday.

ACTION ON THE READING

Gather a group of half a dozen men and women from your church. Invite them to reflect on their best experiences in education, not connected with formal schooling. See what makes these the "best" experiences. How much has to do with the purpose of the education? the place? the leadership? the people? the content?

Is that kind of education happening for any of you right now?

Is any of it happening at your church?

Plan together to make such a learning experience happen in your church within the next couple of months.

CHAPTER THREE

What Is the Second-hour Format?

The approaches to adult education explored here are more
pastoral than prophetic. And they should be.

WORSHIP, STUDY, ACTION

Not very long ago many churches would have been pleased if they could report that the
men's and women's Bible classes were well attended each Sunday morning. Some still are.
But now more and more congregations are beginning to offer both multiple topics and
multiple forms of adult education. Forms range from weekday breakfast classes to workplace
discussions to weekend retreats, and topics range not only from the psalms to the parables
but also from the right to life to the right to die.

Whatever the context, however, no form seems more full of opportunity for most
congregations than the second hour on Sunday morning. It can attract a wide audience, it
can begin with a contemporary issue and move through the heritage of the church, or it can
begin with the heritage and come up to the present. It can be a one-time session or a series,
and it can be the basis for any number of spin-offs.

A Time

Viewed as a block of time, the second hour is approximately an hour-long period for study
on Sunday morning which *follows* the worship service. When the worship hour is ten o'clock,
for instance, the second hour can be at eleven (or, more realistically, at eleven-fifteen). For a
variety of reasons, discussed below, this is probably the best arrangement of all. Not all the
advantages of the second hour are lost when it has to shift away from this preferred schedule
and be offered either before worship or between two services. But the dynamics will change
somewhat when the study hour becomes a preparation for worship rather than a response to
it, or when a class is composed of a mixed group, some having been to the first service and
others planning to go to a later one.

A Relationship

The second hour is more than a time; it is also a relationship. At one level it is related to
one's experience of worship, at another to one's life in a covenant community.

In the most fundamental way, worship always comes before study. Worship is a person's
response to the spirit of God which is revealed in the world and within one's self. It is not at
first intellectual or academic; it is an expression of faith. Yet worship does not happen in
isolation from the rest of life. It should inevitably lead to a time for critical reflection and to a
search for understanding. In a programmatic way, that may be easiest to reinforce when the
second hour (of study) follows the first hour (of worship) on the church's calendar for the

week. Yet even when the worship hour is at eleven or when there are two Sunday morning services, so that the second hour is not second chronologically, study still remains second in priority. Not only does it follow this week's service of worship, it also follows last week's as well, plus a succession of other such worship experiences over a person's lifetime.

If one thinks of the pattern of Christian life as an ever-renewing circle, such a relationship might be described as worship—study—action . . . and then again, worship—study—action, indefinitely.

In addition, the second-hour class has a special relationship to the life of the covenant community in which it is offered.

Recall that covenants have a long history, dating back some four thousand years to ancient Mesopotamia and from there developing into the central metaphor for the relationships which governed much of public life in ancient Israel. Different from a contract, which fosters independence and limited liability between partners, covenant fosters interdependence and accountability between partners. That is true among congregations now as it was for the ancient societies described in Scripture. "Just as God limits the exercise of His omnipotence by entering into covenants with humanity, thereby endowing people with freedom, so too does covenant [among God's people] limit the exercise of the boundless self . . . for the common good" (Elazar and Kincaid, p. 5).

What makes the experience of covenant significant for learners in the second-hour class becomes clear as we recognize that "the plausibility of the ideas we come to accept as true" has a direct relationship to "the social condition in which [those] ideas arise" (Sider, p. 191). It makes a great difference for us as Christians that this "social condition" is the covenant community. Covenant is the context in which the Word is heard, in which it is interpreted, in which it is challenged, in which it is lived out. In that covenant world each of us is free, yet each of us is also accountable to others. In that world, too, there is both risk and hope.

Anyone who recalls Yahweh's struggle to build a faithful community through the prophetic life of Hosea will have some sense of both the risk and the commitment which lie at the heart of genuine covenant. Yahweh has extended himself to the outcast through this story of Hosea and Gomer, of whom he speaks with great love and great faith:

> Therefore, behold, I will allure her,
> and bring her into the wilderness,
> and speak tenderly to her . . .
> And I will betroth you to me for ever; I will betroth you to me in righteousness and in justice, in steadfast love, and in mercy. I will betroth you to me in faithfulness; and you shall know the Lord.
>
> (Hosea 2:14, 19-20 RSV)

Such a covenant relationship provides the ideal context in which the Christian church can invite its members to grow and learn.

ADVANTAGES AND DISADVANTAGES

Men and women learn in church in all sorts of ways: as they share in a baptism or a confirmation, as they canvass members for a stewardship campaign, as they listen to a sermon, as they serve on boards or committees. Much of that learning simply happens, however; it is unintentional, unplanned. When education for adults is part of a structured program, learning moments become educational moments (Hainer, p. 5). As one of those "moments," the second hour on a Sunday morning offers many advantages and only a few disadvantages.

Advantages

At the simplest level, to begin with, people are already at church when the second-hour class is scheduled to start. No one needs to come on a special day or even to come early on a Sunday morning. There is no need to compete with evening activities that range from piano recitals to basketball games to deacons' meetings. If friends and members plan to come to the worship service, they can stay for the second-hour class. Certainly that is an advantage.

But something much more profound than mere convenience is also involved when learning for adults is scheduled at this hour—something that is both psychologically and theologically sound. Scattered people will have already gathered for worship; ideally, in the process they will have become united in a community focused on God. Together they will have shared the spiritual uplift of prayer and praise. It is this experience itself, first of all, that they will then seek to understand. And it is also from this experience that they will go forth, seeking to understand and to serve the world.

In addition, meeting at the second hour offers the optimum in both flexibility and continuity of scheduling. The same time slot is available every week, throughout the year, so that people can get into the habit of attending every week if they wish. Yet because courses can be offered in such varied formats—from one-time sessions to semester-long studies—persons are also free to choose those courses or workshops that most appeal to them. Programs that run from three to six weeks often seem best of all, in their combination of variety with some thoroughness. No one is locked in for a long period who does not wish to be, and newcomers can enter easily without seeming to intrude into a fixed group. Issues can be planned well in advance for careful balance yet be changed almost at a moment's notice when something in the life of the church or community warrants it. All but the smallest churches may also wish to have more than one group meeting at the same time and offering a wide variety of topics appealing to the interests of different persons.

This short-term programming has another built-in advantage, one that can be especially important in a society in which so many persons experience separateness and loneliness and alienation. Not far beneath the veneer of many parishioners, one suspects, is a man or woman who has felt something akin to what the late Dag Hammarskjöld described in these lines:

What I ask for is absurd: that life shall have a meaning.
What I strive for is impossible: that my life shall acquire a meaning.
I dare not believe, I do not see how I shall ever be able to believe: that I am not alone.

(Hammarskjöld, p. 86)

Or maybe they will have felt the sort of pain that a young poet shared with me not long ago from his private journal: "I sit in the snow and contemplate the inadequacy of all former solid grounds. I have lost my personal God. I am unsure of love, what it is and how it works and feels. I am sick; my stomach yearns and turns. And the nourishment it seeks is spiritual."

Less poetically, but no less significantly, we should be aware that to the degree that our churches are a reflection of the larger society, our congregations are also more than twice as likely to include single-parent households than they were only a decade ago.

How can a second-hour class help such a range of persons?

Because it not only groups but regroups its participants according to their personal interests, the second-hour class allows the formation of a network of clusters among groups of church members who might otherwise remain separate: choir members, newcomers, deacons, ethnic groups, single parents, the bereaved, the widowed—the list is endless. Most churches, small as well as large, are made up of such clusters of persons which hardly change from year to year, and that can limit rather than foster a sense of community. It is all too easy, in fact, for them to lead to divisions rather than to unity.

Those who plan second-hour courses would also do well to keep in mind the conclusions of a California study which reported that "almost half of those over sixty" who take part in continuing education classes—whether in church or not—"said that a primary motivation for their participation in learning programs was to meet new people" (Peterson, p. 85). The goal should be a network of cells, always fluid, always shifting . . . and always enlarging the sense that the church is a convenant community.

Finally, the second-hour class—when it follows worship—comes at exactly the right time for two-way participation. Even those sermons that provide the most food for thought are almost always structured as one-way communications; they need talking out afterward. And not only do the sermons themselves need talking out, so do the listeners. A church which seeks to be truly a covenant community needs to provide opportunities for the lonely learners and the quiet learners to hear and to be heard.

Listen as a sixty-year-old man describes how such a study group has opened a new dimension in his life.

"I've always loved to study. Since college days that has most often always meant reading by myself, usually in bed at night after the house got quiet. That's still true, I guess, but it's been different these last three years since my wife died. Instead of reading partly to escape the confusion of the household, as I used to, now I often find myself reading in order to fill a quiet space.

"I confess, I've become something of a lonely learner.

"Something's been happening lately, though, that's opened up a whole new world for me. I'm becoming a part of a learning community again. And it's been happening at church."

The man who shared these thoughts with me is not the only one in our churches who is lonely, of course, nor is he the only one who has discovered a new dimension of his life in the church. No doubt his experience could be matched by that of many others, some only half his age.

What is significant about both him and the others, however, is that their horizons have widened as they have studied in a group. And the key, it should be pointed out, is not so much the studying as it is the group (Williams, "Lonely Learners," p. 31).

Disadvantages

Like any other approach, of course, the second-hour format is not without its apparent disadvantages, although some of them can doubtless be turned into advantages with a little foresight. Two have to do with the time period itself: that it is too short to accomplish enough, and that it is too busy to allow people to arrive on time if at all.

It is true that at second-hour time many adults will be busy with other after-church activities, from simply visiting with friends to conducting the kind of informal church business that always seems to get accomplished best then. But an adult series that addresses the needs and interests of the congregation—or, more likely, of a certain part of it—will attract its own loyal participants. And if some never arrive at all, those responsible for the program should simply assume that they were probably doing things which mattered more. Some, of course, might never have come anyway. But anyone can always attend later on when a different study topic motivates involvement.

Another issue concerns the leadership of the group. Clergy who would wish to conduct such a group, or even to be major resource persons for it, are likely to be under more pressure on Sunday morning than at any other time of the week. In fact, leading a class would hardly be easier for them after the service than before. Thus it may be better for them to participate most often in other settings: on a weekday evening, on a retreat, or in an intensive Advent or Lenten series.

But the pastor, as a teacher of adults, does not necessarily have a special advantage over others in the church. Yes, he or she has certain kinds of professional training and experience that could be very useful at times. Probably no one else in the congregation has as much seminary education, for example. But in most churches there is a much larger pool of potential group leaders to draw from than many persons recognize, each one with special skills and resources. Consider these examples.

A businessperson or travel agent who has recently been to the Middle East might lead a class on the missionary journeys of Paul. A lawyer might explore the justice issues she works with every day in relation to the themes of justice in the Old Testament prophets. A career military officer might teach a unit on the price of peace versus the price of war. The organist might teach a class on Advent or Easter music. But be forewarned: once lay men and women become teachers and discussion leaders, the change may well influence not only the class but, in a very special way, the teachers themselves. Are their self-images as partners in ministry likely to be brightened? Will they be more sensitive about what it means to teach well, more ready with questions, more active? Will they be better prepared at classes other

43

than their own? For most such persons, my experience makes clear, the answers are clearly yes (Williams, "Who, Me," p. 31).

But even more may change than the individual teachers. To change one part of an organization is necessarily to change the rest of it. Will there be a more active laity? More input about the kinds of courses offered? Something closer to genuinely mutual ministry? All this and more is possible when Christians make the designation about the Ephesian church their own: "His [gift was] that some should be . . . teachers" (Ephesians 4:11 RSV) (ibid.).

WHO COMES TO THE SECOND HOUR?

Adults Who Are Different

It is easy to look at a group of men and women who gather at church on Sunday morning and to see them as pretty much alike. According to the social make-up of the congregation, they may seem to be not only all adults but all middle-class or all farmers or all students. This is especially easy given the Sunday-go-to-meeting dress code we usually impose on ourselves. But underneath our three-piece suits and fur collars are unique persons with unique needs. Not long ago the editor of *Joint Educational Development: Share* reflected on those who might be in an adult class like those we have been thinking about:

* ★ an old man "seeking friendship, cherishing a few moments away from the burden of caring for an invalid wife";
* ★ a young mother "looking for intellectual stimulation, above the level of her two- and five-year-old children";
* ★ a couple "with divergent perspectives on religion, hoping for a place to share and compare ideas";
* ★ a widow "expecting the support and security of traditional faith" (Koenig, p. 32).

While this list suggests a wide range of possible ages in the group, the evidence is clear that we should expect two groups to predominate in our classes as in our worship life: women and the elderly. Women of all ages make up a high proportion of those enrolled in continuing education courses outside the church. In fact, they are the nation's fastest growing group of postsecondary students. Why? Some need a base for job advancement or career change for economic reasons. For others a new, more positive self-image makes them able to risk seeking additional education.

Some of these same women will be on the front row of the second-hour class too, yet it is older rather than younger women who should be expected there, including those who are leading essentially single lives.

Many perceptive studies have been made in recent years of the stages that persons go through in their lives, the best known of them probably either Erik Erikson's academic description of the eight stages of man or the more popular *Passages* by Gail Sheehy. These books are worth studying in detail, since only those who are sensitive to both the needs and the contributions of the congregation at various stages of their lives can hope to plan programs that are appropriate for them. An interesting, brief assessment of the contributions of three major age groups to learning in a Christian community comes from Maria Harris: from older members comes a sense of history and legacy; from middle-aged members, the reality of here and now; and from the younger members, a vision and a hope (Harris, p. 46).

Christians

Second-hour courses will attract some of the same persons who would attend adult education programs outside the church, since, at one level, they may seem to be exploring some of the same concerns: the problems of providing affordable retirement housing in the community, for example, or the urgency of bringing peace to both public and private lives. Some such Sunday-morning offerings may also look much like history, philosophy, or sociology courses. Others may look like self-help courses.

What makes them different, however, is that they are being offered not only for, but within, a particular community of faith. Fundamentally, as Robert Havighurst has written, Christian education takes place "in the worshipping and witnessing community of persons in Christ. This community has a life, a message, and a heritage. It has been brought into being, sustained, and directed by God to continue his reconciling work in Jesus Christ. The gospel is its message; the Holy Spirit its power; love is its mood. . . . Christian education in this context becomes nurture in the fellowship of love" (Havighurst, p. 16).

Described in sociological language, this audience is what Peter Berger calls "a cognitive minority . . . a group of people whose view of the world differs significantly from the one generally taken for granted in their society." What makes them a minority, he explains, is that unlike the large numbers of persons in society who "seem to manage to get along without it quite well," to them "the supernatural is still, or again, a meaningful reality" (Berger, *Rumor,* p. 7).

The Seekers

We have seen already that those who come to second-hour programs seek both information and fellowship. And their motivations do not necessarily stop even there. One writer on the trend toward lifelong learning in the broader culture reports that "the overall picture that emerges from the data on adult motivations for learning is that adults are pragmatic learners who pursue education for its practical utility to them. . . . If we are to serve a 'voluntary' learning force, we will need to understand, better than we do now, the real motivations of adult learners" (Peterson, p. 113).

And what is it that these people seek? Broadly, Peterson summarizes, they are looking for any of three goals:
   ★ to obtain something—a goal orientation;
   ★ to do something—an activity orientation;
   ★ to know something—a knowledge orientation.

45

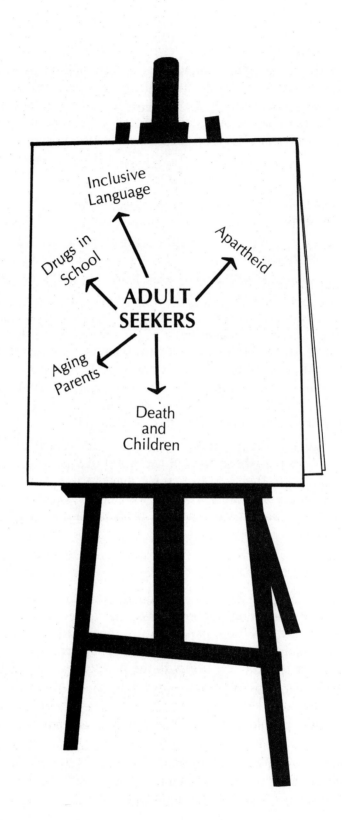

In more personal terms, however, let three laypersons speak for themselves:

★ "I need to start at a level that I can understand, and relate that to me. I need to start with the crazy things that happen in life and learn how I can relate to it as a Christian."

★ "I just need an opportunity to talk with somebody—anybody who'll take me seriously."

★ "I've got a daughter in Sunday school. I guess I ought to know as much about my religion as she does—right?"

The Educationally Successful

We know, too, that those most likely to come are those whose previous successes with education are the greatest. Not surprisingly, they are the ones who wish to return.

BUT WHO DOES NOT COME IS IMPORTANT TOO

Not all those who come to worship regularly will stay to study. Even ideally, the number is more likely to be on the order of twenty percent rather than thirty. What are the reasons why?

Traditional Replies

Some reasons—excuses, maybe?—are so traditional that they can be predicted with ease. Parents are so busy all week long driving their sons and daughters to choir practice or working two jobs that while they may make it to church for the first hour, anything else is asking just too much. Others are disenchanted, perhaps remembering with frustration studies in the past that never quite hit the mark for them, or even remembering with annoyance the teachers or group leaders they never could appreciate. Some are conservative enough that they simply do not wish to change the way they have been doing things for years. They may, of course, have all sorts of needs and interests that could be investigated during the second-hour session, but as long as they sense no needs that the adult education program will meet, they will remain among the absentees.

The Insecure

There is another reason for avoiding the second-hour class, however—probably for many persons the greatest one: insecurity. Fearful of making a mistake, a man or woman may offer "busyness" or "not interested" as a cover for avoiding potential embarrassment. Almost all adults are overachievers in theory, and that can become a high barrier, especially in a middle-class congregation where everyone "knows" that everybody else excels in something.

As one long-time member and church school teacher confessed: "I was afraid to admit how little I knew, afraid I was unable to hold my own in a theological conversation. I felt that other people had a lot more to offer than I did, so usually I just stayed away or otherwise kept quiet."

Learning, we ought not to forget, can be a high-risk venture. It is important, then, that it be offered in a place where it is safe to try, to doubt, and to reveal personal needs. Parker J. Palmer describes this quality as hospitality, explaining, "The reason for hospitable community in the classroom is not to make learning painless, but to make the painful things possible: such things as the exposure of ignorance, the testing of tentative ideas, [and] the mutual criticism of thought" (Palmer, p. 1054).

Learning during the second hour ought to be like that.

Activities for Teachers and Learners

REFLECTION ON THE READING

I. Directions: Listed below are three statements. Review the chapter you have just read to see if it contains the same information that you find here. It does not matter whether the words are identical or are paraphrased, but there must be evidence somewhere in the chapter to support your opinion. Respond to all three statements.

	Agree	Disagree
1. The second hour is both a time and a relationship.	——	——
2. The pastor may not be the best teacher for adults even though she will probably have the best seminary education in the congregation.	——	——
3. The Sunday morning study hour is the wrong place to be an evangelist.	——	——

II. Directions: Read through the following statements and think about how they relate to the information in the preceding chapter. Check each statement which expresses an idea that can be reasonably supported with information from the reading. Be ready to discuss the supporting evidence with another reader.

—— 1. Christian education can't take place under the direction of the League of Women Voters.
—— 2. Christian education should be prophetic before it is pastoral.
—— 3. Unless you've done well in school you probably won't get much out of adult education at church.

III. Directions: Read through the following statements. Think about ideas and experiences you have had which are similar in principle to those you read about in the preceding chapter. Check each statement which you think is reasonable and which you can support by combining ideas in the reading selection with your own related ideas and experiences. Be ready to present evidence from both sources to support your decisions.

—— 1. Without congregational worship in the first hour, there's little chance for successful education in the second hour.
—— 2. Adults don't require schooling to be educated—in church or out.
—— 3. "Birds of a feather flock together"—especially in adult study groups.

ACTION ON THE READING

Make a list of what you regard as the most important dozen or so leadership tasks in your church. Then identify each as either primarily a *laity* task (LT), a *clergy* task (CT), or a *shared* task (ST).

What does your list tell you about the range of educational resource persons available to your congregation?

In addition, add the names of several other members or friends of your church who belong on your resource list.

Finally, compare this list to the names of the men and women who presently teach in your adult program.

CHAPTER FOUR

Now and Then

As Christians we affirm that Jesus is the unique instance
of God's incarnation. Yet each of us is another instance.
The story of God's love and justice is our story too.

THE PAST IN THE PRESENT

In much of our contemporary culture, the past is already out of sight. To claim to be of value, a consumer product must be "state of the art." Even men and women, as the friendly advertisers from Pepsi-Cola used to tell us, must be from the "Now Generation." We live in the present tense, hurtling headlong into a future which we cannot control but which we hope will be less of a disaster than the present. All that is constant is change.

Clichés? Yes, but not without their basis in the rootless realities that describe much of twentieth-century experience. Closer to truth, perhaps, is the observation of novelist Robert Penn Warren that "we Americans—for both good and bad—have a contempt for the past. We set out to make a radically new nation, in all ways, and our successes, beyond all expectation, have encouraged us to agree with Henry Ford that 'history is bunk' " (Williams, "Does the Past," p. 1).

History is bunk? But what about the value of history for us who call ourselves Christians? We are a people with a tradition. Our very identities are tied up in relationships to Abraham and Sarah, to Micah and Amos, to Mary and Jesus and Paul. According to our denominational heritage, moreover, the tradition may continue with Luther or Calvin or Wesley or, more recently, with Martin Luther King.

Even so, few of us, whatever our denominational label, wish to live for very long in the past. In our Christian life we profess to be forward-looking. Not only has God acted in history, we assert, God continues to act in history. And so must we. As early as the Salem Covenant of 1629, for instance, Christians in America were affirming that the will of God had not only been revealed in the past but continues to be revealed in the present. And in our own time the Statement of Faith of the United Church of Christ, to cite just one example, emphasizes a contemporary faith in its present-tense statements about a God who creates and calls and seeks, and about Jesus the Christ who calls and promises—not just in history but, through the Spirit, in the present as well.

Sociologist Peter L. Berger reminds us, "People may like museums, but they are reluctant to live in them" (Berger, *Rumor*, p. 18). Yet conceding that to be true, we must also recognize that in a special way education—whether inside or outside the church—does look to the past, to tradition. "More often than not," in fact, as Robert W. Lynn observes, "we tend to equate education with the dimension of pastness. The work of the educator, according to the casual conventional definition, is to transmit and conserve the best of the past" (Lynn, p. 132).

51

Fortunately, however, Lynn's portrait is an oversimplification. For while it is true that many persons will study a subject or a text that some might call timeless, almost all will expect it to be timely as well. While not overlooking continuity with a great heritage, as H. Richard Niebuhr says, Christian education "must mediate between the heritage and the contemporary situation" (Niebuhr, p. 98). Our challenge is to make the Christian story our own.

In the context of the second hour, this goal can be pursued in three ways: by *telling* the story, by *continuing* the story, and finally by *being* the story.

TELL THE STORY . . . AND MAKE IT OUR OWN

For some persons, stories are something to read to their children at bedtime, or perhaps an escape for adults on a quiet evening. While they may find stories interesting, they do not find them very important. In fact, they could do rather easily without stories altogether.

Others find that there is much more to stories than just a casual way to pass the time. Among other things, these persons sense that the ways we look at life as adults are somehow tied to the stories we were told as children, or to those that we ourselves have read later on.

Some of these would have been children's stories, like Cinderella, with its happily-ever-after ending, or the wonderful animal stories by Thornton W. Burgess with their contagious love for nature. Others were national stories, like the one about George Washington and his cherry tree, or Lincoln studying by firelight, or Martin Luther King proclaiming his dream by the Washington Monument.

Some, certainly, were biblical stories: Abraham and Isaac climbing the mountain to the place of sacrifice, David confronting Goliath with only five smooth stones, the mother of young Samuel presenting him to God at night in the temple, and a whole host of the Jesus stories—his birth in a stable; his encounters with Mary and Martha, Nicodemus, Zacchaeus, and Peter; his triumphant ride on Palm Sunday; his death on a cross; the joy of Easter.

These are not simply favorite stories. To the extent that we become what we read, they are stories that have helped to mold us, to make us what we are. They can also help to make us what we will become.

Now more than ever before, both anthropologists and theologians are paying attention to such stories and to storytelling as well, and as a result some persons may be less likely to discard stories as merely frivolous than they have been in the past. An important influence concerns anyone involved with Christian education: a vital new sense of the ways in which Scripture comes alive in story—for adults in particular, as well as for our children.

Making Sense

At the same time, modern literary critics have been demonstrating convincingly that the meaning of any story—whether biblical or some other—does not lie in the words of the text by

"People may like museums, but they are reluctant to live in them."

—Berger

itself, waiting lifelessly for our exegetical and interpretive scalpels. Nor is it hidden away somewhere in the mind of either its creator or its reader.

Instead, they point out, meaning is continually being created in the tension between text and reader. "Meaning is to be defined," critic Jane Tompkins explains, "in experiential terms. It is what happens to a reader as he negotiates the text and is not something that was already in place before he experienced it" (Tompkins, p. xxiii). Creating meaning is a process, then, in which what we bring to the text is no less important than what the text brings to us.

Moreover, such critics emphasize, readers experience a text not just as individuals but as members of groups whose values and traditions they share. Not only is it true that there can never be a completely neutral reading, there cannot be a completely solitary meaning either. Put still another way, they would insist that readers do not so much *find* the sense of a text as *make* sense of it.

What happens when we examine the Scriptures in this light? At the most fundamental level, they will be seen to have far more than just a past. They have a present and even a future as well. That understanding becomes clear when one considers, for example, how the meanings generated by stories of our heritage of faith are open-ended and alive.

Consider these alternatives. One could affirm, "I believe in God the Father Almighty." Millions of Christians do repeat those very words each time they participate in a service of worship. Or one could tell again the great Genesis story in which the spirit of God sweeps across chaos to create the heavens and the earth, and to create human life. Again one might say, "I believe in the forgiveness of sin." Or one might instead tell the story of Jesus and the adulterous woman—the story that ends with Jesus telling her that he does not condemn her.

The choice here is between the authority of a historic creed and the flexibility of a story which unfolds in new ways with each retelling. One cannot simply extract a moral or a theme or a doctrine from a story without killing the story in the process. So it is with the Scriptures.

From the earliest times, all sorts of religious communities have had stories to tell. But we know that they did not simply retell those tales. They changed them, enlarged them, and put themselves into the story. That was true of the Hebrews of the Old Testament and for the early Christians of the New Testament. And that has not changed for us even now.

Religious education, as Stanley Hauerwas tells us, still "has as its first task the initiation of a community into a story. Its task is not to teach us the meaning of that story but to teach us the story." And he continues, "The task of religious education, therefore, involves the development of skills to help us make the story ours" (Hauerwas, p. 326).

The Example of Psalm 22

Among scores of possible texts that could illustrate how to "make the story ours," let us use Psalm 22 as an example. It is not, of course, a story at all in the obvious sense; it is a lyric and not a narrative. Yet it is a text with a uniquely rich series of contexts which extend not only from the Old Testament to the New but from there through the history of the Christian church.

Picture a study group gathered on a Sunday morning at the second hour to continue a series already in progress on the psalms. Imagine that the group has read Psalms 1 and 19 and that the initial emphasis has been on the psalms as an anthology with both a history and a purpose: it was the worship book of the second temple, drawn from cultic memories that go back at least as far as David. At some point each member of the group will also be asked to compile his or her own mini-anthology of the ten psalms that seem most appropriate for private meditation today, and to share that selection with the group.

Now it is time to consider Psalm 22. The class begins by reading it aloud and trying to make out its general sense.

With a paradoxical combination of faith and lonely despair, the poet of this psalm cries out, "My God, my God, why have you deserted me?" God is no helper to him, the group agrees, as the poem opens. "I call all day, my God" he continues, "but you never answer" (Psalm 22:1-2 JB). Yet still this is his God, and whatever the intensity of his lament, it is not once accompanied with doubt. All he can do is to ask why.

By the end of the poem, however, it is clear that a transformation has taken place. Within the brief time it has taken him to speak these lines, the poet is no longer defeated. He has stopped asking for deliverance. His salvation has already come.

Now what? A class could explore the context out of which the poem comes or the metaphoric language in which it is expressed, or they could compare it to other laments in the psalter which also conclude with praise and affirmation. If merely telling the story were the goal, such approaches might be enough.

But that would be closer to *finding* the sense than to *creating* it in the group.

The psalm is more than simply an artifact of ancient Middle Eastern history to be uncovered, however, and more too than an honored portion of the biblical text. It has a life in the present as well—in our present. As it is read, the text has changed from being an object and has become an event. In the words of Juan Luis Segundo, Scripture is "not a dead letter. It is a word which is incarnated again and again in different situations, different cultures, and different civilizations" (Segundo, p. 33).

For countless Christians, "My God, my God, have you deserted me?" is the anguished cry of Jesus from the cross. That it is in addition the beginning of Psalm 22 may also be significant, to be sure, but it is not so important there as it is in the New Testament. Even the record of Matthew that Jesus said it twenty centuries ago will not, finally, be as meaningful as its ever-new impact on us now as a worshiping community. For us the primary context may well be the three-hour Good Friday service in which the words give voice to the paradox which lies at the very center of human experience: the combination of faith and doubt. It is there that the words come alive, if at all. The issue is not so much *words then* as *meaning now*.

Just as the two sorrowing men who walked the road to Emmaus (Luke 24:13-27) gained hope only when the stranger explained the story to them in the light of their present situation, so the twentieth-century Christian community will gain hope only when we do more than simply listen to the gospel text. We must re-create the text for ourselves. We must share its emotions, be touched by its images—must, as Segundo says, "confront, debate, and transform it . . . must . . .reflect on it, compare it with real life, and see what import [it] has for [our] own concrete existence as individuals, families, and members of a society" (Segundo, p. 32). Only then will we be transformed by it.

How are we to re-create these words for the contemporary church? Where do we direct this second-hour group on the Psalms? To start, one might try to involve the group in a further study of liturgy (an area in which many Christians, lay and clergy alike, are particularly weak) and raise such questions as these:

* ★ What does it mean to have the words read in the context of worship, of celebration?

* ★ What does it mean to read—and hear—during one service the same words from both the psalm and the lips of Jesus: "It is finished"?

* ★ What does it mean to have to wait so long—from Good Friday afternoon to Easter Sunday morning—before being caught up in the fervor of a tightly packed congregation singing triumphantly, "Christ the Lord Is Risen Today"?

* ★ Does the experience of Easter cancel out the realities of being forsaken, or do both feelings coexist?

* ★ What does it mean, further, that we hear the words as members of a community who are in covenant with one another?

These and other questions need to be asked. It will be enough if a group leader asks some of them; members of the group will ask the rest.

But genuine re-creation will require more than just study; it must be a shared experience as well. Picture a group of adults during Holy Week discussing situations which might drive them to utter such a prayer, or situations which had done so already. Then hear them praying the prayer aloud slowly, in unison: "My God . . . why have you forsaken me?" Imagine them, further, reflecting on Jesus' use of these words from his worshiping tradition as a prayer of his own. Do twentieth-century Protestant traditions offer any such liturgical structures? How can such a prayer be one's own personal prayer and at the same time be a distillation in verse of the psalmist's own experience, an expression of Jesus' agony, and a segment of the canonical Scriptures?

And then, later that week, see the group with their friends and families—or perhaps all alone—worshiping at the Good Friday service where the words and the meditation and the study mean something that they have never meant before.

A necessity for Christian education in our time is to go beyond mere antiquarianism in our use and teaching of Scripture, even to go beyond tradition. We must be ready to make sense of the old stories in a new way. Only then will it be clear that when the psalmist cries out, "My God, my God, why have you forsaken me?" he speaks for us.

56

CONTINUE THE STORY . . . AND MAKE IT OUR OWN

The old story, meanwhile, is not the complete story. Our own stories too, both as individuals and as persons seeking to live together in covenant groups, continue as parts of *the* story. And they can also merit a central place in the life of the second-hour class.

Once more, picture a group of men and women gathered on Sunday morning for study and fellowship. This group is composed of leaders, volunteer church visitors, a third of whom have attended the Psalms study; the rest will have come specifically for this workshop. They have come to this workshop seeking help in their task as visitors. They visit with older folks, primarily those who are ill or infirm or bereaved. Some persons they see at home, others in nursing homes.

This second-hour workshop is a time of preparation, where the participants are learning new skills, sharing past experiences, and (since they do their visiting alone) renewing the identity of the group. The dozen or so persons exhibit varying degrees of readiness. Some are eager, others are more quiet. In earlier sessions some have wondered aloud, "What should I say? I don't know all of the folks I've been asked to call on. And I don't always have much in common with them anyway." That has set the agenda for today's meeting.

The leader's role here is not to provide answers to the question, What should I say? from a ready-made list. Rather, it is to invite discussion, to draw on the resources of the group so that members will learn not only with, but from, one another. "How has any one of you been able to break the ice?" the leader asks. "Will somebody describe the way a good visit worked for you recently?"

A Withdrawal from the Memory Bank

Listen as one person tells this story:

"As I walked into the sixty-year-old house, I was attracted almost immediately to an oil painting hanging on the wall. It was one of those classic New England farm scenes—you know the kind, with the white house proud and rectangular and a split rail fence enclosing acres of pastureland.

" 'I like it,' I told the old woman I'd come to call on. And I asked her if the farm was someplace special for her.

" 'Special—oh yes,' she started to say. 'I painted it myself.' And then the floodgates opened. 'That's the old family homestead up in Massachusetts. Why, I have a photograph of that house with my mother out front . . . way back before she was married. Must have been in the 1880s, I guess.' From there she went on with tale after tale, all as fresh in her mind as if they had happened only the day before."

The visitor continues:

"My hostess was a far better talker than she was a listener, I soon discovered. But since, after all, she herself was my reason for staying there for the rest of the hour, I sat back and let her reminisce. In her memory was a wealth of stories—of the one-room school where she had first taught, of her missionary nephew now back in Africa. . . . As I finally stood to leave, she offered 'another installment next time' if I'd have the patience to listen. I promised to come back."

Others in the group follow, contributing their own experiences, agreeing that one of the best approaches for a visitor is to find an opening that invites a person to tell a story about someone who has been important to them in the past and who may also be important to them now.

"But where can a visitor begin?" the leader interjects. "Can we learn some approach that will work for all of us?"

It can be easy, one person points out, if you're at all observant. The crewel work in progress on the couch: "Are you working on a gift for someone?" The open book on the coffee table: "How are you coming on the collection of short stories?" The photograph on the table: "That must be your father. Wasn't he one of the founders of the church?"

For most older persons, someone adds, there will not be as many moments of excitement to look forward to as there are wonderful moments to look backward at. "So let them," she says. "More than that, encourage them. You're not asking them to live in the past, just inviting them to recall it. And remember: they need a visitor to be there so they have somebody to tell those stories to!"

As the conversation moves on, the leader narrows the focus to the visitors' own stories, specifically to stories of their faith journeys. For that, he says, can often be a meaningful part of the conversation with those they visit.

And so each one is asked to draw a simple time-line, plotting on it some of the highs and lows of their own life of faith. Mentally each is to begin the exercise with "I remember . . . " and then try to discover what is in their own memory banks. Highs, it will turn out later, are often times of celebration like confirmation or a wedding or a baptism, or shared experiences on a retreat. Lows are often times away from the church, disagreements with the pastor, or personal tragedies. It will be interesting to discover that tragedies and conflicts, though, are as likely to be considered a high as a low, and for some in the group they will be both at once.

It is not the plotting of the information, however, as much as it is the sharing and interpreting that matters most. Each person finds a partner and interprets the time-line for him or her, and in the exchange, the stories become concrete and visible:

★ sharing in a communion service on the beach at dawn on the last morning of a family retreat on Cape Cod;

★ marching through Times Square in New York City in a crowd of almost a million people, demonstrating for peace and disarmament and singing "We Shall Overcome";

★ feeling cheated at the sudden death of a member of a study group, knowing that he had so much to offer to us as well as others and having no explanation that took away the hurt and the anger;

★ listening to the old gospel songs being sung in Korean by the small group who worship each week in the chapel, bridging time and language and culture.

Our Memory and Our Hope

To say that we are what we remember is to include both the ancient and the more recent stories.

> That story is still unfolding
>   and in faith we make it our own.
> It forms our memory and our hope,
> It tell us who we are and what we are to do.
> To tell it is to declare what we believe.
>   (The Presbyterian Church in the United
>   States, *Declaration*, chap. 1, ¶ 4)

BE THE STORY . . . AND MAKE IT OUR OWN

Finally, after we both tell and continue the story, a second-hour program can also provide support for our quest to *be* the story as well. James R. Schaefer describes the goal well when he asserts that "an evolving educative community is not satisfied with transmitting its culture. It wishes to initiate learners into the dynamics that have been creative of that culture itself so that learners in turn may contribute creatively to the evolution and even transposition of that culture" (Schaefer, p. 39). He is right, of course. Learning to be and to do means far more than merely reciting the facts of the story.

I often find myself thinking of Jesus as what I call "the great for-instance." That is, if the doctrine of the Incarnation is to have any meaning for us today, it will not be that God "came down" in the form of Mary's Son in some magical way but that in Jesus, God is visible in a unique and personal way. It is almost as if Jesus were an acted parable of God. We long for a God who is recognizable, and in Jesus we can sense how God's mystery can be disclosed. But not only do we sense that God is in Jesus; we also discover that Jesus brings out the God who is in us.

As Christians we affirm that Jesus is the unique instance of God's incarnation. Yet each of us is another instance. The story of God's love and justice is our story too.

Admittedly, few things seem so obvious in our post-Christian world as the way in which the experience of the sacred has so often become only a compartment—and a small one at that—of human life. For many persons, the essential goals of life require no church, no faith, no God. Theirs are the words of the popular song of a decade ago, "I did it my way." Yet the Reformed tradition in Christianity affirms that through us the Spirit of God is ready to

59

transform all life. In this view, redemption is not a state of fulfillment in a future life but is the Way toward wholeness in the world around us. Gabriel Fackre wrote some years ago about "engagement evangelism," and that concept continues to be fundamental to the mission of the church. The gospel is something we both tell and do. And it is central to the functioning of adult eduction in the church.

The Ongoing Story

> We confess we are heirs of this whole story.
> We are charged to remember our past,
> to be warned and encouraged by it,
> but not to live it again.
> Now is the time of our testing
> as God's story with the church moves forward through us.
> We are called to live now as God's servants
> in the service of people everywhere.
>
> (The Presbyterian Church in the United
> States, *Declaration,* chap. 7, ¶ 6)

Activities for Teachers and Learners

REFLECTION ON THE READING

I. Directions: Listed below are three statements. Review the chapter you have just read to see if it contains the same information that you find here. It does not matter whether the words are identical or are paraphrased, but there must be evidence somewhere in the chapter to support your opinion. Respond to all three statements.

	Agree	Disagree
1. The work of the educator is to transmit and conserve the best of the past.	——	——
2. All that is constant is change.	——	——
3. Christian educators must help other Christians to *tell* the story, to *continue* the story, and to *be* the story.	——	——

II. Directions: Read through the following statements and think about how they relate to the information in the preceding chapter. Check each statement which expresses an idea that can be reasonably supported with information from the reading. Be ready to discuss the supporting evidence with another reader.

—— 1. Learning at church isn't complete until it changes the way we live.

—— 2. The biblical story is both our memory and our hope.

—— 3. Psalm 22 is about us, when we read it, even though the psalmst couldn't have known that.

III. Directions: Read through the following statements. Think about ideas and experiences you have had which are similar in principle to those you read about in the preceding chapter. Check each statement which you think is reasonable and which you can support by combining ideas in the reading selection with your own related ideas and experiences. Be ready to present evidence from both sources to support your decisions.

—— 1. People may like museums, but they are reluctant to live in them.

—— 2. The experience of Easter does not cancel out the realities of Good Friday—not for Jesus, not for us.

—— 3. We are what we read.

ACTION ON THE READING

Test yourself to see how well you embody the biblical "past" in your own "present." Read the five questions below as if they are your questions; that is, as if each was asked either *by* or *of* you. Try to determine why you are asking the question, or why someone is asking it of you.

WHERE FAITH SEEKS UNDERSTANDING

What are your answers today?

a. "Am I my brother's keeper?" (Genesis 4:9 RSV)
b. "My God, my God, why hast thou forsaken me?" (Psalm 22:1 RSV)
c. "Who is my neighbor?" (Luke 10:29 RSV)
d. "Do you want to be healed?" (John 5:6 RSV)
e. "What must I do to be saved?" (Acts 16:30 RSV)

You may wish to reread the biblical stories from which these questions come.

Now update these old stories so that their themes—and these questions—stay the same but the circumstances are your own. And check once more to see in what ways the ancient story is actually your own.

CHAPTER FIVE

A Word About Teaching

These were persons with special concerns. These were the ones who wanted to solve problems. And about those who stayed away: they must have had other priorities, and that was fine.

MODELS FOR TEACHING

Remember "Show and Tell" from elementary school? Whatever "it" was for the day, one student had it, knew it, showed it, and told it. Everybody else was shown and was told; that was the way they learned. While nobody need deny that the old approach is sometimes still both interesting and useful, we know that for adults it is certainly not enough. Not only does it have the general limitations of being only a one-way communication, it has even greater flaws for specifically Christian education.

Just what does an effective teacher do? The answers are complex, obviously, and varied. But fortunately some models work well for the second-hour class. Three basic premises of these models merit special emphasis: education should be interpersonal, it should be affective as well as cognitive, and it should be based on inquiry.

INTERPERSONAL STYLE

Two educators have offered a theological model for teaching that is interpersonal, contrasting what they see as the Old Covenant way with the New. "*How* we learn," John and Mary Harrell point out,

> is always a concomitant of *what* we learn. The two cannot be separated. From a theological perspective, this principle points to the essential difference between the Old Covenant and the New Covenant. The revelation of God's will by means of law forever confines the revelation in legalism amended by midrash after midrash. The revelation of God in the person of Christ offers the prospect of a living encounter and response of love and forgiveness.
>
> If our teaching more closely resembles giving tablets of law, even if there is an occasional burning bush of inspiration, the *how* limits the *what,* colors it, and becomes an inextricable part of it. If our teaching more closely resembles the personal encounter of the Incarnation, the same process of how with what occurs but with vastly different outcomes (Harrell and Harrell, p. 8).

People may say they want to be informed, and that they appreciate well-informed leaders. But it is essential to guard against overreliance on lecture. Studies continue to show that most students want to be involved too. They want to be not only passive participants but participators too. Peterson cites surveys in which "as many as 70 to 80 percent of the respondents say they would prefer to learn by some method other than classroom lectures," for instance (Peterson, p. 124). Not only does this indicate that there should be discussions, panels, demonstrations, and case studies in classrooms; there should also be more action-oriented learning as well. Providing meals and friendship at an inner city safe house for battered women might follow a workshop on family stress; sharing a Seder meal with some Jewish friends might be the highlight of a course on the eucharist. To such a list, of course, there is no end. What matters in this kind of continuing education is that there be a face-to-face encounter. Some of it will happen during the second-hour session itself; much more will result from it.

Not only should the style be personal, so should the issues. Peace is a priority of my denomination. Reams of materials have been prepared in New York, newsletters are going out, and meetings are being planned in communities across the nation. All this will be helpful, no doubt, as responsible group leaders find available some of the resources they need to deal with their concern.

But merely to work at a national or a global level is not enough. While useful program materials will often come from the top down, the programs themselves will be more successful when their focus is on the local congregation and its surrounding community. The immediate issue at a time of continuing high unemployment in one geographic area, for instance, may be the implications of a reduced arms budget for a church's own members, community, and state. Somewhere else the pivotal issue may be very different. The observation of Donald Rogers is helpful here, when he calls learners "ad hoc utilitarians" (Rogers, *In Praise,* p. 20). People learn best, he maintains, when they sense a need to.

Even when there is no such apparent national consensus that some areas of study and dialogue are timely, the issue of readiness at a local level continues to be paramount. Often it will be evident at major turning points in people's lives: when they are single again, or anticipating retirement, or facing tragedy. Those who plan the program need to find out where people hurt, and then adapt more generalized programs to those particualar needs.

In all of this, meanwhile, one must be sure to keep the focus on faith: on the constant search to find the meaning of faith in the struggles of the world. As one writer maintains, Christian education "seeks to know how the search for meaning relates to learning Christian faith, how the drive for freedom relates to learning moral responsibility, how the desire for security relates to learning and appreciation for redemption, how the need to escape loneliness relates to learning Christian community" (Schaefer, p. 45).

AFFECTIVE AS WELL AS COGNITIVE

Is it only for convenience that we try to separate emotions from things? Perhaps. But feelings are facts too, and the person who would debate over whether to emphasize the affective or the cognitive obscures a basic issue: that education needs both. To minister in the world, Christians need to know the biblical story, remember their heritage and traditions, and understand the needs of the world (cognitive). They also need to develop values, foster a sense of community, and establish a base for ministry (affective). When Christians put these things together by reflecting on what they know and responding to their feelings, they can reach out in love and faith to minister to others.

BASED ON INQUIRY

Christian education in a second-hour format needs to be firmly based on inquiry. If Dwayne Huebner is right when he describes the role of adult education in the church as "developing the reflective conciousness of the total community" (Huebner, p. 127), and I think he is, then there must be a forum in which that reflection is welcome. In addition, that forum must be the place where such reflections can be subject to the loving critique of others in the covenant community. While asking the questions will not always be more appropriate there than learning the answers, the second-hour class offers a place that is open to inquiry and not closed by dogmatic insistence.

Finally, however, let us concede that while many good models of education are available, by themselves they do not begin to be enough. Remembering his many years of professional life as a psychotherapist, Carl Rogers has concluded that "it is the *quality* of the interpersonal encounter"—whether between teacher and student, leader and workshop group, or counselor and client—"which is the most significant element in determining effectiveness" (Rogers, "Interpersonal Relationship," pp. 240-41).

MONROE'S MOTIVATION SEQUENCE

One further model which many teachers find useful has been adapted from skills taught to public speakers. Like others who speak before the public, teachers, as we have already seen, always need to be aware of their audiences as well as their subjects. With this in mind, teachers need to know how to structure their presentations in ways that achieve the best results. Sometimes their goals are largely informational, often they are persuasive, sometimes they call for action. But whatever the goals, the model developed by Alan Monroe can be one of a teacher's best resources. It is both motivation oriented and problem oriented.

The motivation-oriented model has five sequential steps: attention, need, satisfaction, visualization, and action. Here is the way one textbook describes them:

Attention: the creation of interest and desire.
Need: the development of the problem, through an analysis of things wrong in the world and through a relating of those wrongs to individuals' interests, wants, or desires.
Satisfaction: the proposal of a plan of action which will alleviate the problem and satisfy the individuals' interests, wants, or desires.
Visualization: the verbal depiction of the world as it will look if the plan is put into operation.
Action: the final call for personal commitments and deeds.

(Ehninger, et al., pp. 11 ff.)

That may look at first as if it would work better for a lecture than in a more open class employing both questioning and discussion. And a lecture—a speech—is the purpose for which the model was originally developed. But look how helpful it can be when it comes time for a teacher to lead a class.

1. Attention:

I tell the story sometimes of a college student who stood before a speech class with a shoe box in his hand. Taking the top off of the box, he showed his audience that it was filled with leaves, and as he went around the room he asked everyone to reach in and take a single leaf. Once back at the head of the room, and now without saying a word, he reached into his book bag, took out a pair of rubber surgical gloves, and put them on. Only then did he put his hand into the box, pick out a leaf, and hold it up. "Today," he said, looking at his audience with a slight smile, "I would like to ask you a question. Does anyone here know the difference between poison ivy and other kinds of ivy?" Without a doubt, he had their attention.

All too often teachers who think of their presentations as information-centered leap right over this step and simply announce their subject: "This morning we move on to the second letter to the Corinthians. . . ." They would do well to remember the story of the poison ivy and be sure they have the attention of as many persons in their audience as possible.

2. Need:

Adults learn best when they need to solve problems. Christian education leaders should consider those needs when they plan classes for their congregations, of course. But they should also keep the needs in mind as they teach each class. Yes, the adult audience is there in the classroom at least knowing what course topic has been announced, so a teacher can assume that at least some people there care about the issue itself. Others may be in the room for all sorts of different reasons.

But once a teacher *has* their attention, she should then *focus* that attention. At this point a teacher might actually state the need or might prefer to offer an illustration of the need. One might ask persons why they have come. Whatever the technique, the purpose is the same: to relate the subject to the interests of the people in the group before going any farther.

3. Satisfaction:

For some teachers, this middle section may seem as if it is "the class" itself. It is the biblical lesson, the discussion of what causes violence at home, or the sharing of family Christmas traditions. That's what everybody came for, isn't it? Perhaps. But Monroe points out that whatever happens here, it should logically follow from what had been established in the need step before it. One may explain, demonstrate, or give examples . . . but always it is to move to meet the audience's stated needs.

4. Visualization:

This step is most often used in an action-oriented class, when a study group will want to do something with what they have learned. The leader helps the listeners to put themselves into the picture. If the issue is learning to be a better listener at home, adult students can visualize themselves at the breakfast table the next morning. If the issue is doing something to meet low-income housing needs in the suburbs, they can imagine themselves speaking out at the next zoning commission meeting. As Ehninger and Monroe tell their speakers, "You must to the fullest extent possible put your listeners into the picture. Use vivid imagery: make them actually see, hear, taste, or smell the things . . . you describe. The more real you make the projected situation seem, the stronger will be their reaction" (Ehninger, et al., p. 163).

5. Action:

Not every study group calls for action, certainly not every class in every series. Still, a teacher must conclude a class session somehow and will probably want something more

effective than what I call the "Looney Tunes" ending (you know the kind: "That's all, folks!"). Better than that is a deliberate action step: to invite further study or discussion of the subject or to take a particular action. Only then is it time to go home.

This study so far has been primarily theoretical, supported, of course, by a variety of examples from the ministries of many teachers and congregations. Now it is time to go a step further to see how teachers and church school leaders can actually bring such theories to life. The case study that follows shows the path from the genesis of an idea to the completion and evaluation of a short adult course. The procedure here will go from narrative to analysis. The example is from my own ministry.

A CASE STUDY:

How to Tell Children About Death

Background

I'd been listening to the mother of two children one afternoon as she shared her concern about an upcoming family visit that promised to be difficult. Her aged father was planning an extended stay at their house, as he had often done before. But this time things were different: her father was dying. He knew it and she knew it, but the children did not know it . . . not yet, anyway. The question for this mother was not *whether* to tell her children. It would have been impossible for them not to notice their grandfather's infirmity. The question was *how*.

We talked often in the weeks ahead, as the extended family visit was going on. After one such conversation, when she expressed her appreciation that our time together had been helpful, she added, "I just wish that other parents would have the same opportunity. You ought to run a class about it sometime."

Nothing happened immediately as a result of her suggestion. Other classes had been planned for the weeks ahead; so her idea, valuable as it was, was set aside to wait with a handful of other good ideas until the right opportunity appeared.

Meanwhile, though, I began to share with a colleague my concerns about helping parents deal with their children as they faced the reality of death. I discovered—not surprisingly— that he'd known many other families who had faced similar questions of their own. Parents often ask, for instance, if they should bring their children with them to a funeral. Others wonder how they can best help their children deal with the death of a classmate or teacher, or even of a favorite pet. A few parents had faced the death of one of their own children.

There was certainly a need for a class on death education, we agreed, and we decided to present it as a team as soon as we could work it into the program.

What was going on here? First, a matter of individual concern had surfaced in the life of the congregation. Second, it was recognized as being of wider importance within the church community. Only then did it become the subject of a proposed class for adults.

Persons responsible for planning the program decided that it would be helpful—though doubtless painful too—to talk openly about one of our society's last taboos: death. We were prepared to try to address some actual and very pressing personal concerns of parents and of others who work with children. And we hoped, too, that this class might also open some doors to future conversations with the families who would come to these sessions.

Resources

Providing the resources for such a class might have been a problem, but as it turned out, each of us had access to a videotape that we were sure would involve the participants. One of us had a tape showing Dr. Elisabeth Kübler-Ross discussing her work with children and adults who were dying. The other had a brief segment from television's "Sesame Street"—the episode in which Big Bird is told about the death of Mr. Hooper.

These would be useful during our class sessions; we weren't quite sure how yet. But we also wanted to have some follow-up materials and found a valuable resource in the director of our nursery school, who was making a study she called "Learning Together about Death: Using Children's Books to Help Young Children Understand."

To *involve* these parents was a particular goal. There would be helpful information, of course. But we were not nearly as interested in providing facts as in engaging the persons who would come. This was an example of addressing *affective* as well as *cognitive* needs.

Using the videotapes also had at least three advantages: bringing outside resources into our study room, stimulating both sight and sound, and providing for a common response to the video. Since our usual location for such study groups was the church's comfortable living room, we also knew that the participants would be at ease just "watching TV."

We were also concerned about sharing leadership. Because this church both emphasizes and supports professional leadership, we knew that many in the group would have been quite satisfied to have us run the course. We had no problem with that, yet we did want to widen the participation if we could. A highly respected layperson, director of the nursery school for many years, provided the ideal person. She had not only information that was different from ours but also skills and experience as well. It was serendipity at its most welcome that she was completing work on the subject for a university research project right when we needed her.

Promotion

Some persons had already expressed an interest in our offering such a course. Others were interested, we knew, in the ideas the course would deal with. Some of these we spoke to individually. I also told members of a class I was currently teaching what was being scheduled for the weeks ahead and invited them to come. Then I put a notice in the weekly bulletins and ran this announcement in the newsletter:

How to Tell the Children:
A Two-Part Series on Death and Dying

There is little that causes people so much worry, consternation, and anxiety, and is so conscientiously avoided, as the topic of death. Yet, paradoxically, there is nothing so inevitable in our lives as dying.

In elementary schools especially, teachers go to great lengths to keep the subject of death out of the curriculum, as if children were too tender and fragile to deal with the concept. Even dead hamsters are smuggled away on weekends. "If you don't think about it," the reasoning seems to be, "maybe it will go away."

But of course it won't.

If you sometimes wonder "what to tell the children," or if you have other concerns about death and dying, plan to attend this two-part class. With videotape and guided discussion we will explore the issue of death in a positive and Christian way.

The classes would start in about a month, giving people time to plan. Calendars are full and schedules often need to be rearranged. Good communication—some personal, some public—can help to bring the right participants together. Without good promotion, leaders can expect to hear the familiar lament, "If only I'd known about it in time. . . . "

Who Came?

About two dozen persons attended the two sessions—a good group, we thought. Some came as couples, some individually. Some were currently facing a problem of death and dying, some were still working through their grief from a past event, and others hoped to learn how to be ready for the problem when the time came. All were involved with children, either as parents, grandparents, or teachers.

This was an unusual group, quite different from those who could be expected to appear for almost any other study course. One man I had never even met before in my four years in this congregation. Perhaps we had never listened well enough before to find out what his needs were. These were people with special concerns. These were the ones who wanted to solve problems. And about those who stayed away: they must have had other priorities, and that was fine.

The Two Class Sessions

After a very brief welcome and introduction at the first session, we went right to the sharing of a tape, recorded on a member's VCR, of a "Sesame Street" episode. We explained the situation: the actor who played Mr. Hooper had died, so something had to be done in the show to account for that loss. The videotape—only about five minutes long—would show how the producers had made use of the opportunity. (The tape is not available commercially, but

70

readers can use a book, *I'll Miss You, Mr. Hooper,* which reproduces this episode's script almost word for word.)

After it was over, we asked for response. First, did the "Sesame Street" people handle the situation well? Next, would you have done it differently?

It was easy to start that way. Not only was the tape entertaining and professionally done, but using it also kept the emotional and personal issues at arm's length for a little while until we started talking. People would soon begin to involve their own families and to offer their own examples; we knew that. But we wanted that kind of sharing to be their choice and not ours.

Our role as leaders was to stimulate responses and to provide a forum where personal reflection was welcome. We knew that there are those who regard students, including adults, as a "circle of ignorance" surrounding the source of wisdom. But we did not feel that way at all. As one person put it later on, "You're there to be a traffic cop. Without your direction we'd never get to our destination in one piece."

Using videotape instead of film, by the way, had the additional advantage of letting us keep the lights on and thus remain alert to our study-group setting. This was no time to get lost in the world of Big Bird and his friends.

The next week we showed a somewhat longer tape, made on a home VCR, in which Dr. Elisabeth Kübler-Ross described her work. We heard her talk about her experience with dying persons and watched her with both old and young persons themselves. Our directions to the class beforehand were few: only to watch and to respond afterward by sharing how each person felt about the videotape.

Again the advantages of using videotape were clear, but this time the original audience was adults, not children. As we watched Kübler-Ross we were inevitably confronted with our own attitudes toward death.

Kübler-Ross was a familiar name to many in the group, and one of her books, *Death: The Final Stage of Growth,* was in the church library. It was not necessary for anyone to have done any homework, however. We brought the professional resources; they brought themselves and their personal experience.

We had not emphasized before this time that this was a "Christian" discussion of death and dying so that we adults could learn to present the issue "faithfully" to our children. But in this second session the Christian dimension became very obvious in two ways: some persons talked about theological matters relating to a life of the spirit beyond one's physical death; others talked about the support of the church as a community of faith.

Here especially it was clear that the style of learning, as well as its subject, was interpersonal. The open tears on the faces of some persons also showed just how affective (as well as effective) the study was. There was no attempt on the part of anyone, leaders or other adults, to suggest that we had *the* answer. But we all had brought with us both needs and experiences, and they were what we shared in this Christian study group.

As our time grew to a close we called attention to the books on the tables—about two dozen or so. Some were from the town library across the street from the church; they could be borrowed easily. A few were from our own church library; we'd ordered them in time to have them available to any who were interested. And there was an annotated bibliography of many more titles for the benefit of any who wanted to continue their study individually.

The books helped people to come to a closure. This was designed as only a brief study group, and it was about to end. But the issues themselves would not end, and we wanted to offer a bridge to help the participants along their way.

What Were the Lasting Effects?

A young mother stopped me after church the next Sunday. "That class on death and children sure came at the right time," she said. "I came downstairs yesterday morning and found my three-year-old son watching his dead goldfish floating on top of the aquarium. I don't know what I'd have done before the class—probably flushed the thing down the toilet just as soon as he turned away, I guess. But, no, instead we talked about it. I told him the thing had died and then we even buried it in the garden out back. I think that made it easier for him. I know it sure did for me."

She wasn't the only one to take the classes to heart. They had brought back such surprisingly intense memories for me that I wrote pages and pages about them in my journal. Then, a few weeks later, I put those notes together and wrote the following pages. Later they would become a brief article for publication in a national religious magazine:

How to Tell the Children

"Where's Ginger?" our daughter Sherri asked as she hurried down to breakfast. "Did he come back?"

She'd been worried the night before when our eighteen-pound orange cat hadn't come home, and as she climbed the stairs to her room she asked her mother and me to try calling him again before we finally went to sleep. "Promise?" she pleaded; "You won't forget?"

No, we hadn't forgotten. I'd even gone out into the backyard near the woods, but calling didn't help. Ginger wasn't there.

"I wish he was here . . . where he belongs . . . with me," Sherri moped as she put on her sweater and headed off to her kindergarten classroom. "Do you think he'll come back before I get home?"

"Don't worry," I answered optimistically. "We can look for him after school if he's not back by then."

But I remember that her mother and I were concerned ourselves. Ginger had never stayed out all night before, and he always came running whenever he was called. Something must be wrong. Still, we didn't want the children to worry, so we just acted normally. We never put a label on our actions, but psychologists would have called it denial: acting as if the problem would go away if we simply stopped thinking about it.

Late that morning, though, I discovered the truth we'd suspected all along when a neighbor called to ask if our big orange cat was at home. He hoped so, he said, because he'd just seen a cat that looked a lot like ours by the side of the road on the other side of the woods—a dead cat.

Now we knew. Ginger had been run over by a car. He was dead. And he was never coming back.

But how would we tell the children?

Almost before we could think about it, Sherri was home. "Did he come back?" she called out as she ran into the kitchen. "Where is he?"

Because we love our children, we had always tried to protect them from needless pain and tears whenever we could. We didn't just admonish them to watch carefully before crossing the street, to avoid scrapes and bruises and broken bones. We acted in emotional ways too, trying to mend disappointments with hope and to overcome distance with holiday trips to Grandma's.

So almost instinctively I answered, "No, he's not here." And then after a brief pause, I added, "I guess maybe he's run away."

Ginger did not come back, of course. He never would. But after a few days the children stopped calling for him, and before long dinner table conversations weren't dominated any more by almost tearful comments about "that stupid cat" that had run away.

Maybe I had done the right thing after all, telling them what I had, I rationalized. He did run through the woods, didn't he—through the woods to the road where he was hit? And wasn't it better that the children be spared the pain—and the reality—of his violent death? They were so young.

But I had lied.

It was a long while afterward—nearly twenty years later—that Sherri, now a grown woman, brought up the subject of Ginger again. She remembered nostalgically how that cat had put up with a lot of abuse from her and from her younger sister and brother too, how he would let them use him for a pillow while they watched Captain Kangaroo on TV, and how much she had missed him when he "ran away."

Then quietly, she looked up at me and asked, "Why didn't you just tell us he was run over? That's what really happened, isn't it?" When I nodded my head, she added, "We guessed it anyway."

And so we talked . . . about how hard it is for parents to admit that death causes them pain too, and about how important it is that children be helped to face death. We talked about death as an opportunity to be grasped to help even very young children deal with the world around them.

Having learned to deal with the death of a pet like Ginger, for instance, would probably have made it far easier for our children to have dealt later on with the death of a teacher, a classmate, or a grandparent. And those times did come, eventually.

I remembered what I'd heard a hospice counsellor tell an audience of young parents. "You

73

don't have to teach your children about death," he'd said. "They'll learn about it anyway on the playground or on television. And doubtless for most of them it will come sooner rather than later."

With the wisdom of hindsight, as Sherri and I talked, I wondered how I would handle the disappearance—no, the death—of a pet cat differently if I had it to do again? I decided that I'd be guided by five rules:

1. *Be honest.* That means not only avoiding the lie that the pet has merely run away; it also means using language that is honest. Whether it was Ginger or Uncle Ben, the truth is that he *died* rather than *passed away,* that he is *dead* rather than just *gone.* Yes, the truth does often hurt. But an untruth will probably hurt even more.

2. *Deal openly with feelings.* Not only loss but anger and guilt as well are normal responses to death. Children need to know that, need to experience those feelings themselves and to know that "it's O.K." and need to know that in the face of death adults feel pain too.

3. *Listen more than you talk.* Invite your child to talk freely about the pet or the person who has died—to remember the way Ginger raced through the house after he'd played with his catnip mouse, for instance, or the way Grandpa made us all laugh with his animal stories. Death is seldom a good time for explanations, though. You're there to help the grieving process along, not to provide a theological education.

4. *Don't expect the process to be over in a few moments.* It won't be. Young children especially will often cry for a few moments and then run off to play, as if their grief has come and gone. But it will come back, and an alert parent needs to watch for it.

5. And finally, just *be there* for comfort and security. In the face of death a child will often lose trust in the world, and a parent needs to be available to show that life goes on. You can't put Humpty Dumpty together again, it's true, but you can likely manage to scramble the eggs and zip up the jacket.

It still won't be easy to tell the children when someone, or something, they have loved has died. It never is. But I'll know how *not* to start. I won't begin with, "He ran away."

 ## WHAT ELSE?

This article was my response, the goldfish story was someone else's. But what of the rest? It is hard to know. People give what they can and take what they need. I could only think then, as I often do when a course is over, of the parable of the sower. Some seeds, Jesus explained, fell in the rocks and thorns. But other seeds fell into rich soil and produced a rich harvest.

Activities for Teachers and Learners

REFLECTION ON THE READING

I. Directions: Listed below are three statements. Review the chapter you have just read to see if it contains the same information that you find here. It does not matter whether the words are identical or are paraphrased, but there must be evidence somewhere in the chapter to support your opinion. Respond to all three statements.

	Agree	Disagree
1. Adult education should be based on inquiry.	——	——
2. Television is a better learning tool than big-screen movies.	——	——
3. Most adults prefer some other method of learning than a classroom lecture.	——	——

II. Directions: Read through the following statements and think about how they relate to the information in the preceding chapter. Check each statement which expresses an idea that can be reasonably supported with information from the reading. Be ready to discuss the supporting evidence with another reader.

—— 1. The Old Covenant provides a better model for adult Christian education than the New Covenant.

—— 2. Tears on the face of one study group member were evidence of a failure on the teacher's part: he'd caused her to feel pain.

—— 3. What we learn is always tied to how we learn.

III. Directions: Read through the following statements. Think about ideas and experiences you have had which are similar in principle to those you read about in the preceding chapter. Check each statement which you think is reasonable and which you can support by combining ideas in the reading selection with your own related ideas and experiences. Be ready to present evidence from both sources to support your decisions.

—— 1. I'd rather just say, "He's gone to heaven"; that's gentler than saying, "He died." And anyway, I believe it.

—— 2. He ran away.

—— 3. You're the teacher; you ought to know.

ACTION ON THE READING

With two or three others, recall the earliest memories when death became a reality of your life.

a. How old were you?

b. Who or what had died?

 c. How did you feel about it?

 d. Who was there with you to help you work out those feelings?

 e. Was anyone at your church or church school helpful to you then?

 f. How would it have helped if you'd had something to read, written especially for kids?

Talk to the children's librarian at your town library to see what's available for children about death and dying. Next, arrange to have the best three or four titles added to the collection in your church library. And then publicize the fact that they are ready to be borrowed.

CHAPTER SIX

A Brief Course for Teachers and Leaders

What difference does it make to be in this study group
rather than in one sponsored by a local college?

What would happen if the ideas and principles which have been described in these pages were put to the test in the local church? More specifically, what would happen if they became the basis for a second-hour study group in *your* church? One way to arrive at some answers for yourself is to offer a course of study like the sample class on the KKK described in the preface.

Such a course on Sunday mornings will be a shared experience, an opportunity for women and men in your congregation to be a part of an active/reflective kind of learning. Members of your church community will, of course, have already participated in various learning activities as Christian adults. Now they will have an opportunity to reflect on those experiences. Afterward, some will be ready to proceed to further continuing education and, one would hope, toward a new dimension of mutual ministry as well. After the experience of the course, the participants will be better informed about the values and opportunities of second-hour studies.

Although any interested persons should be invited to attend (perhaps the course should simply be promoted as another in the customary range of your adult education offerings), it might be especially valuable for members of the congregation's Christian Education Committee, particularly for those on the subcommittee responsible for the adult education program.

A preliminary teaching outline for a four-week study series follows. As shown here, the first three sessions are offered as a unit. The fourth session should be separated by enough time that members of the class will be able to participate in the next regularly-scheduled course.

If possible, the first three sessions should be held on Sunday mornings at the second hour, following the worship service, in a lounge where participants can sit in a circle on comfortable chairs. The fourth session should meet at a different time and place, probably some evening when more time is available, and in a somewhat more formal setting such as the church's library or a classroom, where everyone can sit around a conference table.

The course might also be offered in an all-day retreat format where it would be the center of the agenda and thus not have to compete with other classes and activities. Those who started in the morning could be expected to remain throughout the day. A time of evaluation would be important several weeks after the retreat to give persons an opportunity to reflect on how they have applied their learning.

This outline, it should be noted, is not a substitute for a complete lesson plan identifying goals, objectives, and resources. Each teacher will need to develop that sort of plan, whether formal or informal. (This may, by the way, be an appropriate place to practice using the motivated sequence.) This is primarily a *question outline*, with a few comments added about the leader's procedures or response.

Adults Ought to Know Better: A Study Series for Adults

THE FIRST SESSION

1. If people don't know one another, especially if there are newcomers, take a moment to get acquainted. Be sure everyone knows who you are. Make them feel welcome.

2. Ask each person, first, to look back to the "best" experience he or she ever had in adult education at church, and second, to decide what made it best. (If you are using the motivated sequence, consider this your attention step.)
   Procedure:
   a. Jot the two responses down briefly on a card or pad (have some handy, along with some extra pencils).
   b. Next tell a partner (preferably someone in the group you don't know very well) about what you've written. Take four or five minutes for this part—time enough for some details to surface.
   c. Then ask the group for a quick listing of their responses so that you can put them on a pad of newsprint. Each answer is important because each person is important; don't leave anyone out.

3. Now invite them to look more carefully at the answers they've been talking about. Do their responses suggest any of the reasons why they have come to this place on this particular morning? Are there different reasons why others might have come? (This begins your need step.)

4. At this point you may want to introduce some of the terminology of learning theory. If so, do it as a way to categorize the group's own answers.
   a. Cognitive reasons: to learn something
   b. Affective reasons: to experience something
      (1) the experience of learning itself
      (2) being with other learners
      (3) being with other church members
      (4) "a compulsion" to be here if there's a class

78

5. Especially if this is a small group, ask them why they think others are not present.
   a. Don't offer them any suggestions initially; they'll have many of their own.
   b. You may wish to add one or more of these later, if your group does not mention them: too busy? small children? general lack of interest? sense of risk involved?

6. Do their answers indicate anything about the ways in which *adults* learn (as contrasted to the ways in which *children* learn)? (This begins your satisfaction step.)
   a. Emphasize the personal and practical dimensions of their answers. A person in one of my study groups answered: "We want to do something with what we learn."

7. Ask how conscious they are that they're learning here—right now—as part of a community of faith. What are the characteristics of that community? Does it matter that they've come here right after worship? What difference does it make to be in this study group rather than in one sponsored by a local college?
   a. Quote Sider: "The plausibility of ideas depends on the social support they have" (Sider, p. 191).

8. Don't be overly concerned if you don't finish all the questions or if you end on an unfinished note. Remind your class of the questions you've asked and invite them back next week for more.

THE SECOND SESSION

1. Begin with a quick review, using last week's pad of newsprint as your guide.
   a. *Why* you're here: cognitive reasons, affective reasons, adult reasons. Point out an example or two of each type.
   b. It makes good sense that you *want* to learn and *enjoy* learning.
   c. This is *Christian* education.

2. Today's focus: that we learn as part of a community of faith.

3. Read in unison a historic creed or the statement of faith of your denomination—whatever is the one *most familiar* to your class.
   a. For example, here is the original Statement of Faith of the United Church of Christ.

   NOTE: A later version of the Statement of Faith with inclusive language is used in UCC worship.

   We believe in God, the Eternal Spirit, Father of our Lord Jesus Christ and our father, and to his deeds we testify:

   He calls the worlds into being,
   creates man in his own image,
   and sets before him the ways of life and death.

   He seeks in holy love to save all people from aimlessness and sin.

   He judges men and nations by his righteous will declared through prophets and apostles.

   In Jesus Christ, the man of Nazareth, our crucified and risen Lord,
   he has come to us
   and shared our common lot,

conquering sin and death
and reconciling the world to himself.

He bestows upon us his Holy Spirit,
creating and renewing the church of Jesus Christ,
binding in covenant faithful people of all ages, tongues, and races.

He calls us into his church
to accept the cost and joy of discipleship,
to be his servants in the service of men,
to proclaim the gospel to all the world
and resist the powers of evil,
to share in Christ's baptism and eat at his table,
to join him in his passion and victory.

He promises to all who trust him
forgiveness of sins and fullness of grace,
courage in the struggle for justice and peace,
his presence in trial and rejoicing,
and eternal life in his kingdom which has no end.

Blessing and honor, glory and power be unto him. Amen.

Procedure:

a. Do not discuss the reading or ask, for instance, whether people understand it or agree with it. Just quietly assert instead that everyone present comes to this class from the tradition(s) reflected in the statement. That is "our faith"; we have come here for the "understanding."

4. Ask *what* a community like yours—that is, like the one reflected in the creed or statement of faith—should expect to study here on Sunday morning.

a. Some answers you could expect, but here again don't supply them as leader. Your task is inquiry, not response—at least at first.

b. But be ready with some follow-ups:

(1) Where did the statement come from? Who does it represent? How did it get into the back of our hymnals? Why do we read it in the worship service?

(2) What room is there for a person in this church to be critical of the statement (or parts of it)? How does it "judge" the one who reads it? Does acceptance or rejection brand a person as an insider or outsider?

5. Ask *how* a community like this should expect to study. (Here begins the visualization step.)

Procedure:

Offer three choices for discussion.

a. Inquiry?

(1) Khoobyar: purpose of adult education is "to encourage adults to seek answers to their own questions" (Khoobyar, p. 21).

(2) Tillich: "Man cannot receive an answer to a question he has not asked" (Khoobyar, p. 50).

b. Lecture?

c. Discussion?

NOTE: Be prepared for a consensus that they're looking for "lecture-plus." Many in the group will probably want the leader to be a "teacher," that is, an authority figure who is also the source of facts. "Discussion" will likely be acceptable to most of them; yet several people will probably make it clear that they came for a sense of certainty that only a teacher/professional can supply. They'll gladly discuss the material and even apply it, if possible. But many won't feel ready to go home without this vertical sense of assurance.

6. For next week, ask the class to come with a list of questions that they think *ought* to be investigated in an adult study group. (The visualization continues.)

THE THIRD SESSION

1. Review: What's been happening here?

   a. "Learning" vs. "schooling" for adults

   b. Learning in a Christian community

   c. Style: benevolent dictatorship? republican leadership? democratic town meeting?

   d. Goals: informational? relational? problem-solving?

2. Inquiry: Ask members of the class to identify (on three-by-five-inch cards, which you should provide) three questions that are being asked by members of this church—or, if you prefer, specifically by study group members—questions that could be the basis of an adult study series.

   NOTE: Those who remembered to do last week's assignment will have come prepared. But some may have forgotten and others may be present who missed the week before.

3. Are any of these questions being explored in church study groups already, or have they been the subject of study recently?

   a. If yes, were you part of the class?

4. Would you participate in a class that did study any of these issues? If yes, at what time? in what format? with what leadership? If no, why not?

5. A final point: application.

   a. See if the group agrees that adult education in church is more than making withdrawals from the library of Christian tradition.

   (1) Do they know the three-step meaning of the word *praxis*: experience . . . reflection . . . application . . . (and back to experience).

   (2) "If you *continue* in my word, you are truly my disciples" (John 8:31 RSV, emphasis added).

   b. Do they understand "mutual ministry" as the goal, or is information its own end?

   (1) Both inside and outside the congregation?

   (2) Remember Niebuhr: the end of ministry is "to increase the love of God and neighbor." Is that also the end of Christian education?

   c. You may want to suggest examples from the recent life of your congregation. For instance:

(1) Did a study of the international peace movement change any relationships at home or at work?

(2) Did a study of the apocryphal Gospel of Thomas change the way you read, or use, the four canonical Gospels?

(3) Did a study of apartheid in South Africa change the way you invest in the stock market or the way you choose consumer products for your family?

THE FOURTH SESSION

This last class can be the most flexible of all, since the members who have participated in all of them will have gained considerable ownership of the study. It may be enough to work from this three-part outline, or add to it whatever your group suggests is appropriate.

1. Review the fundamental premise of the course: faith/worship first; then seeking for understanding.

   a. Do you act yourself into believing or believe yourself into acting?

2. Four questions for evaluation tonight:

   a. Which courses (or other learning experiences) in the church this year have meant the most to you?

   b. In what formats?

   c. What—and who—have been the resources?

   d. Do any of us see our ministry as more effective because of our participation in any of these classes (including this theoretical one)?

3. And finally, your action step: where do we go from here?

Activities for Teachers and Learners

REFLECTION ON THE READING

I. Directions: Listed below are three statements. Review the chapter you have just read to see if it contains the same information that you find here. It does not matter whether the words are identical or are paraphrased, but there must be evidence somewhere in the chapter to support your opinion. Respond to all three statements.

	Agree	Disagree
1. Adults who study for *cognitive* reasons want to learn something.	——	——
2. Adults who study for *affective* reasons want to do something.	——	——
3. We learn as part of a community of faith.	——	——

II. Directions: Read through the following statements and think about how they relate to the information in the preceding chapter. Check each statement which expresses an idea that can be reasonably supported with information from the reading. Be ready to discuss the supporting evidence with another reader.

——1. Historic church creeds and more recent statements of faith define for their users what it is to be Christian.

——2. Making a question outline is a good way to prepare for teaching a class.

——3. Adults who've had a good learning experience are likely to remember something about their teacher and about the other learners, not just the information they learned.

III. Directions: Read through the following statements. Think about ideas and experiences you have had which are similar in principle to those you read about in the preceding chapter. Check each statement which you think is reasonable and which you can support by combining ideas in the reading selection with your own related ideas and experiences. Be ready to present evidence from both sources to support your decisions.

—— 1. A person cannot receive an answer to a question she has not asked.

—— 2. *We* believe in God, the Father almighty. . . .

—— 3. Adults ought to know better.

ACTION ON THE READING

Share this proposed course outline with others in your congregation who are committed to strengthening your adult education program. Revise it to make it fit your people and their needs as you understand them. Choose someone to be the group leader, maybe yourself. Publicize it.

And then teach it.

Postscript

The challenge and the opportunity to educate adults beckons in our churches.

We all have much to learn and, to paraphrase the words of Robert Frost, we have miles to go before we sleep.

M.G.W.

Bibliography

Agnew, Marie. *Future Shapes of Adult Religious Education*. New York: Paulist, 1976.

Anderson, James D., and Ezra Earl Jones. *The Management of Ministry*. New York: Harper, 1978.

Apps, Jerold W. *How to Improve Adult Education in Your Church*. Minneapolis, Minn.: Augsburg, 1972.

Berger, Peter L. *A Rumor of Angels*. Garden City, N.Y.: Doubleday, 1969.

————. *The Sacred Canopy: Elements of a Sociological Theory of Religion*. Garden City, N.Y.: Doubleday, 1967.

Bergevin, Paul. *A Philosophy for Adult Education*. New York: Seabury, 1967.

Bergevin, Paul, Dwight Morris, and Robert M. Smith. *Adult Education Procedures: A Handbook of Tested Patterns for Effective Participation*. New York: Seabury, 1963.

Berton, Pierre. *The Comfortable Pew*. Philadelphia: Lippincott, 1965.

Bowman, Locke E., Jr. *Teaching Today: The Church's First Ministry*. Philadelphia: Westminster, 1980.

Brim, Orville G., Jr., and Stanton Wheeler. *Socialization After Childhood: Two Essays*. New York: John Wiley, 1966.

Broholm, Dick, and John Hoffman. *Empowering Laity for Their Full Ministry: Nine Blocking Enabling Forces*. Edited and revised by Janet Madore. Newton Centre, Mass.: Andover Newton Theological School, 1981.

Broholm, Richard R. "Toward Claiming and Identifying Our Ministry in the Workplace." *Laity Project Newsletter* 3 (Spring/Summer 1982), pp. 1-12.

Brueggemann, Walter. "Covenant as a Subversive Paradigm." *Christian Century* 96 (November 12, 1980), pp. 1094-99.

Brundage, Donald. *Adult Learning Principles and Their Application to Program Planning.* Ontario: The Ministry of Education, 1980.

Bucy, Ralph D. *The New Laity: Between Church and World.* Waco, Tex.: Word, 1978.

Chartier, Jan. "Becoming Effective Teachers: A Process Guide for Leaders of Adult Groups." *JED: Share* (1978).

Colby, Richard E., and Charity Weymouth. In "Shared Ministry: Lay Leadership Development." *Small Churches Are Beautiful,* edited by Jackson W. Carroll, pp. 94-105. New York: Harper, 1977.

Cross, Patricia, Alan Tough, and Rita Weathersby. *Adults as Learners.* San Francisco: Jossey-Bass, 1977.

DeBoy, James J., Jr. *Getting Started in Adult Religious Education.* New York: Paulist, 1979.

Diehl, William. "Monday Morning Ministry." *A.D.* (July-August 1982), pp. 12-14.

Dudley, Carl S. *Where Have All Our People Gone?* New York: Pilgrim, 1979.

Ehninger, Douglas, Bruce E. Gronbeck, Ray E. McKerrow, and Alan H. Monroe. *Principles and Types of Speech Communication.* 10th ed. Glenview, Ill.: Scott Foresman, 1986.

Elazar, Daniel J., and John Kincaid. "Covenant and Polity." *New Conversations: Polity and Practice* (Fall 1979).

Elias, John L. *Conscientization and DeSchooling: Friere's and Illich's Proposals for Reshaping Society.* Philadelphia: Westminster, 1976.

Erikson, Erik H., ed. *Adulthood.* New York: W. W. Norton, 1976.

Ernsberger, David J. *Education for Renewal.* Philadelphia: Westminster, 1965.

Evans, Gary T., and Richard E. Hayes. *Equipping God's People: Basic Concepts for Adult Education.* New York: Seabury, 1979.

Fenhagen, James C. *Mutual Ministry: New Vitality for the Local Church.* New York: Seabury, 1977.

Fish, Stanley E. "Literature in the Reader." In *Reader-Response Criticism,* edited by Jane P. Tompkins. Baltimore: Johns Hopkins, 1980.

Freire, Paulo. *Pedagogy of the Oppressed.* New York: Seabury, 1970.

Hainer, Frank T. "The Learning Milieu of the Church and the Ecology of the Adult Christian Mind." *Nexus Note* No. 101 (The Program Agency, United Presbyterian Church), March 15, 1982.

Hammarskjöld, Dag. *Markings.* Translated by Leif Sjöberg and W. H. Auden. New York: Knopf, 1964.

Harrell, John, and Mary Harrell. "Modes of Learning." *JED: Share* (Summer 1980), pp. 7-8.

Harris, Maria, ed. *Parish Religious Education: The People, the Place, the Profession.* New York: Paulist, 1978.

Hauerwas, Stanley. "The Gesture of Truthful Story: Religious Education." *Encounter: Creative Theological Scholarship* 43 (Autumn 1982), pp. 319-86.

Havighurst, Robert J. *The Educational Mission of the Church.* Philadelphia: Westminster, 1965.

Havighurst, Robert J., and B. Orr. *Adult Education and Adult Needs.* Syracuse, N.Y.: Syracuse University Press, 1956.

Herber, Harold L. *Teaching Reading in Content Areas.* 2nd ed. Englewood Cliffs, N.J.: Prentice-Hall, 1978.

Hesburgh, Theodore M., Paul A. Miller, and Clifton R. Wharton, Jr., eds. *Patterns for Lifelong Learning.* San Francisco: Jossey-Bass, 1974.

Hessel, Dieter T. "Continuing Education of Adults in the Church: A Critical Overview with Constructive Proposals." *Nexus Note* No. 102 (The Program Agency, United Presbyterian Church), March 15, 1982.

Hill, Jocelyn. *Adult Workshop Manual.* Atlanta: General Assembly Mission Board, Presbyterian Church in the United States, 1980.

Hoge, Dean R., and David A. Roozen, eds. *Understanding Church Growth and Decline: 1950-1978.* New York: Pilgrim, 1979.

Holmes, Urban T. *Spirituality for Ministry.* New York: Harper, 1982.

Houle, Cyril. *The Design of Education.* San Francisco: Jossey-Bass, 1972.

Howe, Michael, ed. *Adult Learning.* New York: Wiley, 1971.

Huebner, Dwayne. "Education in the Church." *Andover Newton Quarterly* 12 (January 1972), p. 124.

Keeton, Morris T. "Dilemmas in Accrediting Off-Campus Learning." In *The Expanded Campus: Current Issues in Higher Education 1972,* edited by D. W. Vermilye, pp. 139-148. San Francisco: Jossey-Bass, 1972.

Khoobyar, Helen. *Facing Adult Problems in Christian Education.* Philadelphia: Westminster, 1968.

Knowles, Malcolm. *The Adult Learner: A Neglected Species.* Houston: Gulf, 1973.

———. *Modern Practice of Adult Education.* Rev. ed. New York: Association Press, 1980.

———. *Self-Directed Learning.* New York: Association Press, 1975.

Knox, Alan. *Adult Development and Learning.* San Francisco: Jossey-Bass, 1977.

Koenig, Norma. Editorial. *JED: Share* (Summer 1980), p. 32.

Levinson, Daniel J. *The Seasons in a Man's Life.* New York: Knopf, 1978.

Lewis, Douglass. "The Dimensions of Faith." Hartford, Conn. 1975. Typed handout.

Leypoldt, Martha M. *Forty Ways to Teach in Groups.* Valley Forge, Pa.: Judson, 1967.

———. *Learning Is Change: Adult Education in the Church.* Valley Forge, Pa.: Judson, 1971.

Lynn, Robert W. "Sometimes on Sundays: Reflections on Images of the Future in American Education." *Andover Newton Quarterly* 12 (January 1972), p. 132.

McCarthy, Estelle Rountree. *Adults: A Manual for Christian Education—Shared Approaches.* Atlanta: General Assembly Mission Board, Presbyterian Church in the United States, 1977.

McCullough, Charles R. *Morality of Power: A Notebook on Christian Education for Social Change.* New York: United Church Press, 1977.

McKenzie, Leon. *The Adult Learner: A Neglected Species.* Houston: Gulf, 1974.

———. *Adult Religious Education: The 20th Century Challenge.* West Mystic, Conn.: Twenty-Third Publications.

———. *Creative Learning for Adults: The Why/How/Now of Games and Exercises.* West Mystic, Conn.: Twenty-Third Publications, 1977.

Marty, Martin E. "The Sunday School: Battered Survivor." *Christian Century* 96 (June 4-11, 1980), pp. 634-36.

Maslow, Abraham H. *Motivation and Personality.* 2nd ed. New York: Harper, 1970.

Metzger, Roscoe F. "First Congregational Church in Bloomfield: Property and Buildings, 1858-1978." Privately printed in Bloomfield, Connecticut, 1978.

Moran, Gabriel. *Education Toward Adulthood: Religion and Lifelong Learning.* New York: Paulist, 1979.

Mouw, Richard J. *Called to Holy Worldliness.* Philadelphia: Fortress, 1980.

Niebuhr, H. Richard. *The Purpose of the Church and Its Ministry.* New York: Harper, 1977.

Noreen, David S. *Priorities for Adult Education.* Chicago: Department of Christian Education, The Evangelical Covenant Church of America, 1977.

Ong, Walter J. *The Presence of the Word.* New Haven, Conn.: Yale University Press, 1967.

Palmer, Parker J. "Truth Is Personal: A Deeply Christian Education." *Christian Century* 97 (October 21, 1981), pp. 1051-55.

Peters, John, et al. *Building an Effective Adult Education Enterprise.* San Francisco: Jossey-Bass, 1980.

Peterson, Richard E., et al. *Lifelong Learning in America.* San Francisco: Jossey-Bass, 1980.

Posner, George J., and Alan N. Rudnitsky. *Course Design: A Guide to Curriculum Development for Teachers.* 2nd ed. New York: Longman, 1982.

Prather, Hugh. *Notes to Myself.* Moab, Utah: Real People Press, 1970.

Presbyterian Church in the United States. *A Declaration of Faith.* Atlanta, 1977. Pamphlet.

"Presbyterian Panel Findings: The April 1982 Questionnaire—Adult Christian Learning." *Nexus Note* No. 126 (The Program Agency, United Presbyterian Church), December 20, 1982.

Rogers, Carl R. *Freedom to Learn.* Columbus, Ohio: Merrill, 1969.

———. "The Interpersonal Relationship: The Core of Guidance." In *Bridges, Not Walls,* edited by John Stewart, pp. 249-48. 2nd ed. Reading, Mass.: Addison-Wesley, 1977.

Rogers, Donald B. *In Praise of Learning.* Nashville: Abingdon, 1980.

Ross, Elisabeth Kübler. *Death: The Final Stage of Growth.* Englewood Cliffs, N.J.: Prentice-Hall, 1975.

Sangiuliano, Iris. *In Her Time*. New York: Morrow Quill, 1980.

Schaefer, James R. *Program Planning for Adult Christian Education*. New York: Newman, 1972.

Segundo, Juan Luis. *The Sacraments Today*. Maryknoll, N.Y.: Orbis, 1974.

"Seminar Report: Toward the Task of Sound Teaching in the United Church of Christ." n. p., n. d. Mimeograph.

Sheehy, Gail. *Passages: Predictable Crises of Adult Life*. New York: E. P. Dutton, 1977.

Sider, Ronald J. *Rich Christians in an Age of Hunger: A Biblical Study*. Downer's Grove, Ill.: Inter-Varsity Press, 1977.

Smythe, Ormond. "Practical Experience and the Liberal Arts: A Philosophical Perspective." In *Enriching the Liberal Arts Through Experiential Learning,* edited by Stevens E. Brooks et al., pp. 1-12. New Directions for Experiential Learning, no. 6. San Francisco: Jossey-Bass, 1979.

Stiles, Norman. *I'll Miss You, Mr. Hooper*. New York: Random House/Children's Television Workshop, 1984.

Taylor, Marvin J., ed. *Foundations for Christian Education in an Era of Change*. Nashville: Abingdon, 1976.

Tompkins, Jane P. "An Introduction to Reader-Response Criticism." In *Reader-Response Criticism: From Formalism to Post-Structuralism,* edited by Jane P. Tompkins, pp. ix-xxvi. Baltimore: Johns Hopkins, 1980.

Tough, Allen. *The Adult's Learning Projects*. 2nd ed. Austin: Learning Concepts, 1979.

United Church of Christ. *The Constitution and Bylaws, United Church of Christ*. Pamphlet.
———. *Resolutions of the Annual Meeting, October 1985, The Connecticut Conference of the United Church of Christ*. Hartford, Conn.: Connecticut Conference of the United Church of Christ, 1985.

Vos, Nelvin. *Monday's Ministries*. Philadelphia: Fortress, 1977.

Warren, Roland L. *The Community in America*. 3rd ed. Chicago: Rand McNally, 1978.

Westerhoff, John H. III. *Will Our Children Have Faith?* New York: Seabury, 1977.
———, ed. *A Colloquy on Christian Education*. Philadelphia: Pilgrim, 1972.

Wheeler, Barbara. "Continuing Education in the Church Education System: A Dim View." *The Auburn News* (Spring 1983), pp. 1-5.

Williams, Melvin G. "Does the Past Have a Future?" *Dialogue for English Teachers in West Virginia* 9 (Spring 1977), pp. 1-2.
———. "Lonely Learners." *Baptist Leader* (April 1985), p. 31.
———. "Making Sense: What Happens When You Read?" *English Journal* (April 1986), pp. 33-35.
———. "On the Laity." *The Congregationalist* 135, no. 3 (March 1975), pp. 7-9.
———. "Who, Me—A Teacher?" *Baptist Leader* (March 1985), p. 31.

BIBLIOGRAPHY

Wink, Walter. *The Bible in Human Transformation*. Philadelphia: Fortress, 1973.
————. *Transforming Bible Study*. New York: Abingdon, 1980.

Zuck, Roy B., and Gene A. Getz, eds. *Adult Education in the Church*. Chicago: Moody, 1970.